Popular Mechanics

SHED NATION

DESIGN, BUILD & CUSTOMIZE
THE PERFECT SHED FOR YOUR YARD

DAN ECKSTEIN

HEARST BOOKS
A division of Sterling Publishing Co., Inc.

New York / London
www.sterlingpublishing.com

Special thanks to Better Barns, LLC (www.betterbarnsandsheds.com)

Design by Liana Zamora

Library of Congress Cataloging-in-Publication Data

Eckstein, Dan, 1966-
 Shed nation : design, build, and customize the perfect shed for your
yard / Dan Eckstein.
    p. cm.
 "Popular Mechanics."
 Includes index.
 ISBN 978-1-58816-712-5
 1. Sheds--Design and construction--Amateurs' manuals. I. Popular mechanics
(Chicago, Ill. : 1959) II. Title. III. Title: Popular mechanics shed nation.
 TH4962.E25 2010
 690'.892--dc22
                            2009026572

10 9 8 7 6 5 4 3 2 1

Published by Hearst Books
A division of Sterling Publishing Co., Inc.
387 Park Avenue South, New York, NY 10016

Popular Mechanics is a registered trademark of Hearst Communications, Inc.

www.popularmechanics.com

For information about custom editions, special sales, premium and corporate
purchases, please contact Sterling Special Sales Department at 800-805-5489
or specialsales@sterlingpublishing.com.

Distributed in Canada by Sterling Publishing
c/o Canadian Manda Group, 165 Dufferin Street
Toronto, Ontario, Canada M6K 3H6

Distributed in Australia by Capricorn Link (Australia) Pty. Ltd.
P.O. Box 704, Windsor, NSW 2756 Australia

Manufactured in China

Sterling ISBN 978-1-58816-712-5

I would like to thank: my editor at Hearst Books, Alyssa Smith, for her steady hand, her patience, and her grace under deadline pressure; my agent and guardian angel, Stephany Evans, for her guidance regarding the intricacies of the publishing world; my colleague, Dave Warren, whose encyclopedic knowledge of carpentry and building, and his generous willingness to share it with me, proved valuable beyond words; my wife, Tara, and son, Noah, who provided the essential love, encouragement, and space to keep me moving forward; and to the entire Yestermorrow Design/Build School community, whose passion for designing, building, teaching and learning about beautiful, durable, and environmentally sound structures and communities is a never-ending source of inspiration.

Homeowners know there's no such thing as enough storage space. There's a limit to the things you can squirrel away in your basement and garage. Sometimes what you really need is a garden shed—one large enough to house an arsenal of outdoor power tools while providing organized space for everything from rakes and shovels to fertilizer and fuel. But if you don't want to just pick up a pre-fab shed from the parking lot of a home center, what then?

Planning and building a shed or barn can be an ideal opportunity to express yourself in a very creative way. It's the ultimate hands-on project—a chance to lay claim to the territory out the back door. After all, sheds offer far more than utilitarian storage space. They can become whatever you need: a greenhouse, a workshop, a sanctuary, or even a reflection of your personality.

If you're the type of person who dreams up plans at the kitchen table and then heads for the stacks of 2 x 4s and plywood to build something truly original, this is the book for you. Learn how to draft plans that will pass building codes; figure out what kind of siding and trim best complements your house; and decide which custom elements you'd like to see on your outbuilding. With *Shed Nation* by your side, you'll have the hardworking, practical information you need to design, build, and customize exactly the building you want in your yard.

Don't spend more time spinning dreams—make them a reality with the help of *Shed Nation*.

The Editors
Popular Mechanics

When it comes to yards and lawns, America is a nation of perfectionists. For the homeowner, the yard is a statement about everything from one's artistic sensibilities to one's ability to create order from chaos. It provides the opportunity to 'be' the landscape architect, organic vegetable farmer, or Chicago Cubs groundskeeper you always dreamed of being.

Not sure whether you're in the club? Do you tend the lawn like a manicurist? Do you plant shrubs and bushes and ornamental trees in the perfect locations, and then move them when you realize the first site was not quite so perfect? Do you landscape and sculpt with stone and brick? Do you rake and mow and edge and clip?

America is also a nation of accumulators. Our basements, attics, and garages are filled to overflowing with shop tools, snow tires, memorabilia, lampshades, and camping gear. From the potting and planting supplies you use each summer, to the tiles left over from that bathroom flooring project, to the toys and games the kids long since outgrew, there's no denying the quantity of stuff that clogs our homes.

It is these very reasons, these yard and possession obsessions, that drive another dynamic desire—to own one's very own shed. In fact, perfect lawns and overflowing garages almost demand them.

We love sheds for their utility. They not only allow us to stash some of our excess stuff, but also give us the opportunity to get organized. In them, we can store garden and yard equipment (mowers, rakes, shovels), recreational gear (bikes, skis, sleds, kayaks), or lumber and tools (ladders, two-by-fours, table saws). Thinking beyond storage, sheds can provide usable workspace. A workbench lets you put those tools to use. A potting bench provides a place to plant seedlings and flowers for the garden. Windows or skylights with southern exposure may provide the option for a small greenhouse to give those seedlings a head start.

We also love sheds because they allow us to make an architectural statement that most of us can only minimally make with our home. Most people buy or build a house based on affordability, location, and functionality. Aesthetics are of course important, but they sometimes end up taking a back seat to the first three criteria. But with a shed, the relatively diminutive scale and cost allow us to design and build the structure we'd love to live in but don't, be it a stately colonial, a rustic gambrel farm barn, or a funky Adirondack-style lodge. Your shed both houses the tools that help you make your yard beautiful, and adorns the yard itself with its very existence, providing a focal point, a design statement that informs the rest of your landscaping choices.

Building a shed also provides the opportunity to expand your knowledge and skill set, to perhaps work together with family and friends, and to gain the elemental satisfaction of standing back and looking at the structure you just built with your own hands. A shed's size is a perfect starting point for an aspiring DIYer. It is small enough that it will not overwhelm you with complexity and

scale, nor require that you bust your budget on tools and materials, but it's meaty enough to give you a sizeable taste for what it means to build big.

Beyond the next page is your passport to become a resident of Shed Nation. The following chapters provide a step-by-step guide detailing how to design and build the shed of your dreams. You'll learn how to site your shed in the most attractive and most useful location, how to design a space that works for your needs, and how to choose the materials that will stand the test of time and look great, too.

You'll get a crash course in carpentry and structural anatomy, in nailing roof shingles, and in building a workbench and trimming a window. You'll learn what tools you need, what shortcuts to take (and not take), and when you're in over your head.

Finally, you'll see examples of all sorts of sheds and outbuildings—from the mundane to the fanciful. Some will inspire you, some will educate you, and some will make you chuckle. And most of them were designed and built not by professional builders and architects, but by people like you, armed with little more than some basic tools, a bit of know-how, a dream, and the impetus to make that dream a reality.

Now you've got the same impetus. It's in your hands. Just turn the page and get going.

CHAPTER 1

Planning
and
Design

You've convinced yourself that
you need a shed. Now what?

Utility

Before you visit the hardware store, take out a pad of paper and a pencil. Designing your new shed will begin with a list detailing its potential uses, and there are many. Will it become a workspace or primarily used to store a lawnmower? Will it need to be heated? Begin by writing everything down.

→ **STORAGE** If you plan to use your new shed for storage, list the major items you hope to stash there. Take a walk through your basement, attic, and garage, taking note of the specific clutter you would ideally relocate.

→ **WORKSPACE** Perhaps your new structure will be a workspace: for potting plants and flowers to smarten up the patio and for starting seedlings for the vegetable garden, or for doing small woodworking projects, or for your spouse's mosaic creations or other artistic impulses.

→ **PLAYHOUSE** Perhaps the space will be a playhouse or hideout for the kids. What will capture their imagination? You could create a gingerbread house, a fort, or a tree house.

→ **CABANA OR SAUNA** If you have a pool, you might need a changing hut or cabana—or perhaps a sauna or hot tub enclosure to foster your much-needed relaxation and peace of mind.

→ **WOODSHED** If you have a woodstove or fireplace, your new structure could act as a woodshed for next winter's firewood.

→ **MULTI TASKER** More than likely, your shed will need to perform on several of these fronts, as a mixed-use space. Fill your list with each and every use and write down the predominant items to be stored there.

Siting

Now that you are clear on the structure's function(s), you are ready to begin considering its location. This is one of three critical criteria for determining your shed's site. The other two are aesthetics, and zoning and other regulations.

▶ SITING FOR FUNCTION

Your intended use for the shed is a driving factor in where you site it. Clearly if you are using the shed as a pool house, it needs to be near the pool, and if you are using it as a garden shed, put it near the vegetable garden. But if it is a multi-purpose structure, perhaps storing both garden equipment and firewood, this decision becomes complicated. If its site is next to the garden, but 200 yards from the woodstove in the house, each time you trudge through the snow with an armload of logs, you'll regret your decision.

If you hope to set up your table saw and router in the shed, you will obviously require electricity. Consider the distance and route by which that power will travel, whether underground or via extension cord. Siting the shed on the far side of the rose bushes, across the stream and down the steep embankment could be impractical at best, and a money drain at worst, as digging hundreds of yards of trench to lay conduit or erecting utility poles is onerous and potentially expensive work. On the other hand, your spouse may be thrilled by the distance and reduced noise pollution.

For the snow blower, how far from the driveway do you really want to be? Kids' playhouse? Likely near enough the house to hear the cry from a hurt knee or hurt feelings, but far

(right) This garden shed is mere steps from the perennials.

enough to give them a sense of independence. Bikes, golf clubs, skis? Close enough to the driveway for easy access but not so close that the car will get scratched every time you open the shed door.

Even if your property is measured in feet rather than acres, you have siting options. Tucking the shed in the far back corner is often the instinctual placement, to minimize its impact and keep the lawn unobstructed for ball games and cookouts. But don't discount a more prominent location next to the garden, or adjacent to the swing set, or on the far side of the driveway—again, depending on its potential functions.

For better or worse, a building in your yard is going to be a focal point so make it stand out from its surroundings as you intend.

You can forget about the Japanese garden and koi pond. Forget the neat rows of apple, pear, or peach trees. Forget the perfectly manicured golf putting green. The visitor's eye—and yours—will inevitably be drawn to your shed. That doesn't mean you should hide it behind a hedgerow so it won't be a distraction; it means you need to think about how the shed can work with, or even accentuate, your yard and garden's features.

The dance between the natural environment and the built environment is a complicated one—complicated enough to allow landscape architects to make a good living. But as with most professions there are usually some essential, commonsense kernels of truth that guide a sensible approach.

→ **INTEGRATION.** Think about a house in your neighborhood with absolutely no landscaping around it. Every neighborhood has one. It could be a fabulously beautiful structure, but without something framing it—trees, bushes, shrubs, a garden fence—it looks strange. A shed in the middle of an open field will suffer from the same problem.

You need to integrate your shed into your yard. Accomplish this after the fact by planting shrubs or building a garden fence, or begin the process before you build. Start by looking at your yard's existing features.

→ **EDGES.** Push the shed's potential site from the yard center towards its edge, where there might be some vegetation to act as a backdrop. Placing the shed near a tall tree, flower bed, or other flora can provide the balance your shed needs. Avoid pushing the shed out of the yard completely, however: You'll need to do far more site prep in untended trees and bushes, especially if you break ground for foundation work or leveling and run into tree roots. Additionally, lack of sun due to too many overhanging trees can lead to wood rot and mossy roofs as the shed may never get to dry out after a good rain.

→ **ALIGNMENT.** A shed placed at an off angle (relative to the main house) can appear informal, while constructing your shed parallel to your home will maintain an image of order and tidiness. Alternatively, there is the option of tying the shed into a previously designed

---

SHED NATION CITIZEN

This studio is 12 x 16 feet and sits on a row of 8-inch concrete blocks laid on top of an existing rough slab. I poured a 4-inch-thick concrete floor inside. I used precut two by fours spaced on 16-inch centers for framing, and made the roof trusses using 10-foot-long two by sixes at a 12 in 12 pitch. A 45° cut on the rafters' peak made the trusses easy to fabricate and resulted in very little waste. The exterior siding is wood paneling that I painted. I decided to use a metal roof

which turned out to be easy to install. To keep out the Michigan winters, I installed batt insulation and finished the inside with ⅜-inch plywood paneling. My wife and I are very pleased with the studio.
—ROBERT GREEN, Plainwell, MI

feature such as a vegetable or flower garden, a patio, or stone path. Your shed can also act as a partition between different parts of your yard, or between your yard and your neighbor's. If you have a fence line that partitions your property, you can place the shed against it and construct doors on both sides, creating a gateway from one side of the fence to the other.

Whatever limitations your yard presents, look for opportunities to make your shed relate to the natural and man-made elements around it. And if your lot offers no opportunities for creative aesthetic siting, don't be afraid to opt for the do-the-least-harm strategy and stash it in the yard corner.

One important recommend-ation: If your potential shed site is anywhere near a neighbor's

Window boxes and a cheerful blue door integrates this shed and wood pile storage into this homeowner's yard.

house or yard, make a courtesy visit to let them know your plans. It's your yard and you can do with it as you like, but talk with them anyway. How would you feel if you came home from work one day to find your neighbor had dropped a shed directly in front of the sunset view from your patio? Communicating with, and including, your neighbors will be important in this process.

Finally, get outside and walk your property. Walk to all the potential sites and visualize the structure in its spot. Picture the shed's potential effects on the landscape, both pro and con.

MAKE YOUR WORLD

The act of designing and enclosing space can be transforming. I have witnessed it time and again. Technically shy people who had previously assumed that the world must be as given, become suddenly and profoundly aware that there is no rule or reason for accepting things as found. If you put pencil to graph paper, and put hammer in hand, and ultimately put up four walls, however timidly at first, then nothing can stop you from putting up any number of walls, with windows, doors, roofs, dormers, decks - there are no limits. It's simply a matter of degree and a shed is the perfect first step. We can make our world.
—*JOHN CONNELL, architect, author, founder of the Yestermorrow Design/Build School*

Once you have considered your shed's location based on its function and aesthetics, check in with your town or local municipality to see whether there are any zoning requirements, restrictions, or regulations that might dictate the structure's site and size. Many towns have setback requirements that demand that structures be a certain distance from property lines, roads, other structures, wells, septic systems and leach fields, streams, ponds or wet areas. You may be required to draw up a sketch of the property, indicating the major features and the proposed shed location along with distances to and from various boundaries and items. Don't worry about creating a work of art. It just needs to be clear and functional.

Many towns expect you to submit and pay for a building permit, though the cost is usually minimal. The permit fee is usually a percentage of the building's value or size, which means in most cases it will be under $100, or nothing at all if below a certain square-footage threshold—usually 100 or 120 square feet.

Many municipalities want detailed construction documents if the structure will be larger than a certain square-footage threshold—often 200 or 250 square feet. These are meant to assure the building inspector that the structure will be sound and not pose a danger to you or neighbors. Your plans will be judged according to local, state, or national building codes, and the building inspector's biggest concerns are the foundation method and materials (see chapter 2) as well as the size and spacing of floor joists, wall studs and roof rafters, and the thickness of the decking material and roof sheathing (see chapters 2 and 3). The inclusion of electricity, heat, or plumbing in your structure may raise regulatory interest regardless of the building's size.

Towns will often require a permanent foundation (piers or other footings) if the structure will be larger than 200 square feet. Very diligent inspectors may want to pay a visit to the site after the foundation has been set as well as when the building is complete, to ensure you have built a structure that conforms to the size, location, and construction methods expressed in your permit.

So before sliding that shovel into the ground, head directly to the town offices (or check them out via online records) to find out exactly what the requirements are and what all the steps of the permitting process may be in your town.

This garden shed serves double use as a workroom.

Designing a Shed

You've thought about your shed's function, assessed its aesthetics , and considered your town's zoning restrictions and requirements. And finally, you've settled on the perfect site. Now comes the fun part. What exactly is your shed going to look like? Take a look at some common architectural styles to determine which one appeals to you best.

▶ ARCHITECTURAL STYLES

Buildings are classified by their architectural style, which is determined by their appearance and structure, the materials used, and the historic period in which they were originally built. Additional characteristics might include: the roof pitch and shape; window and door sizes, placement and shape; the decorative details; and the building's size, shape, and interior floor plan. Here's a quick rundown of some of the more common North American varieties.

→ **COLONIAL.** The classic New England Colonial home is two stories, white or un-painted, with a door in the direct center of the building. The roof is fairly steep, with side gables. The colonial house is square or rectangular, with symmetrical windows and a chimney running through the middle of the building to maximize indoor heating. Generally built of wood, it has wood clapboards or shingles on its exterior.

→ **TUDOR.** Tudor refers to a style of English-Gothic architecture popular during the Tudor period (1485–1603), often characterized by half-timbered house exteriors, complex roofs with numerous gables, large groups of rectangular windows, bay windows, and patterned brickwork. The interiors feature richly wood-paneled walls and the lavish use of molded plasterwork to decorate walls, ceilings, and cornices.

→ **VICTORIAN.** Generally built between 1860 and 1900, the Victorian style spread rapidly with a variety of distinctive sub-styles emerging, including Gothic Revival, Italianate, Mansard, Queen Anne, and Folk Victorian. Some common characteristics of Victorian architecture are bay windows, stairs to the front door, and cone shaped turrets. It is also common to have horizontal ridges at the roof line and above each window.

→ **CONTEMPORARY.** Contemporary homes can feature a wide variety of design features and aesthetic values, but in most cases they are homes built in the late 20th century with an emphasis on angular or irregular shapes, expansive windows, a lack of ornamentation, modern architectural lines, open floor plans, and lower-pitched roofs.

(left) This classic Tudor provides ample storage opportunities. (right) Attractive wood paneling adorns this simple shed.

Elements of a Shed

It's time to make some simple choices that will turn your shed into a worthy addition to your yard. Some careful decisions about the roof style, siding material, windows, doors, decorative details, and color choice can mean the difference between attractive and eyesore. As for functionality, you've already done much of the work you need to in this regard. You've considered the uses of the space and the items it will house, as well as its optimum location, so now there are just a few more decisions: its size, internal organization, and door and window placement.

▶ SIZE

One of the most critical design decisions is to determine the appropriate size and shape of the structure. A stunning 4 x 6 foot shed that only stores half of what you had intended is not functional. The other half will either remain in the basement or get stuffed into the shed anyway. A 500-square-foot barn with vast, unused space wastes money and materials, not to mention overwhelming your backyard landscape.

Determining the size that fits your needs and budget requires a quick drawing exercise. Get yourself a pencil with a good eraser, a couple of sheets of graph paper, a tape measure, and the list you created earlier detailing the shed's purposes and functions. If you plan to use the shed mainly for storage, head down to the basement, up to the attic, into the closets, and under the back deck, and take measurements of every major thing you intend to store in your shed. Measure height, depth, and width and write them down. Double check your list; you don't want to forget a big-ticket item.

Then draw a rectangle on your graph paper. This will be a conceptual floor plan, or bird's eye view, of your shed from directly above. Use a scale of $1/2$ inch = 1 foot. If you have a pre-conceived notion of what size you might need, sketch that. If you have no idea what scale will fit your needs, start with an 8 x 12 foot rectangle, which is the size of a typical, medium-sized shed. Once you've got your rectangle drawn, fill it in with the dimensions of your items (bags of potting soil, bikes, outdoor furniture, ladders, the snow blower, wheelbarrow). Don't worry about making your sketches pretty; all you need are labeled squares, ovals and rectangles that are dimensionally accurate. For smaller items, sketch in an area for shelves. Make sure they are deep enough to function for the items they will hold. The critical, but oft-forgotten, task is to be sure to factor in enough clearance around each item so you will be able to easily move things in and out.

If the shed will be used for tasks instead of, or in addition to, storage, think about the space and equipment required for those tasks. How much room do you need on a potting bench to fit your seedling trays? How much space does your table saw take up, in addition to the area necessary for the infeed and outfeed of lumber? Can the outfeed go out the opened shed door? How far away from your easel do you need to be to get a distant perspective on your watercolor masterpiece?

(right) Two doors and shelves for storage make the most out of this multipurpose use shed's space.

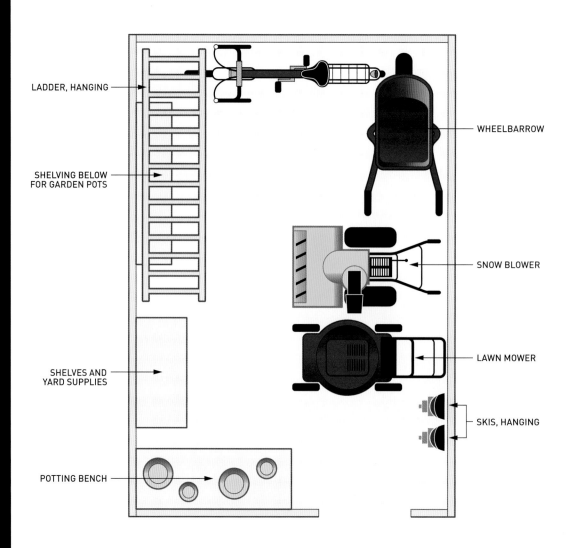

LADDER, HANGING

SHELVING BELOW
FOR GARDEN POTS

SHELVES AND
YARD SUPPLIES

POTTING BENCH

WHEELBARROW

SNOW BLOWER

LAWN MOWER

SKIS, HANGING

Feel free to move items and workspaces around, trying out different arrangements. If you can't fit it all in, expand the shed's dimensions using your eraser.

When you have a concept of the size, visit your shed's future site with some stakes and string and measure out the footprint. Stand in it and visualize moving the lawn mower in and out, or hanging the bikes from the ceiling joists. Does it fit comfortably on the site, or does it block the vegetable garden's morning sun?

Sketching out the space needed for storage and work will insure you build the right size shed for your needs. Don't feel pressure to illustrate your riding mower exactly. Simple circles and ovals will serve for this sketch.

Once you've determined the appropriate size you'll need to think about shape. Consider both interior functionality, exterior aesthetics, and building material usage.

As a rule of thumb, perfect squares can result in a hard-to-access dead zone in the middle. Rectangles, especially with a short wall to long wall ratio of between 1:2 and 3:4, offer pleasant and functional proportions. An area of 100 square feet could translate to a 10 × 10 square, or a rectangle of 8 × 12 (96 sq. ft.), or 6 × 16 (also 96 sq. ft.), or even 7.25 × 13.75

(99.69 sq. ft.). This last option will be wasteful and costly because lumber and other building materials often come in 4-foot or 8-foot dimensions, which means less cutting and less leftover material if your structure is based to some extent on a multiple of those. The 6 × 16 option could work if the site demanded it, but its elongated proportions will likely provide storage and function challenges. The square could also work, but its inherent aesthetic and functional dead space make it less than preferable. For these various reasons, 8 × 12 hits the mark,

as would 4 × 6, 5 × 8, 6 × 10, 10 × 16, or something in that ballpark.

As for exterior frontage, the question is how much shed you want visible from wherever it will most likely be seen, and the effect that frontage will have on the surroundings. A 16-foot face may make an overwhelming statement compared to the 6 x 6 herb garden directly in front of it. Or the 4-foot front face of a 4 x 8 shed might be dwarfed by the Goliath-sized lilac bush adjacent to it. If you hope to use the sun for light or warmth, you will need a south-facing wall with windows, and that wall would ideally be the longer dimension to maximize the light.

Shape might also be dictated by something as simple as the space limitations of the site. Fences, an oak tree, or a rise or fall of the topography might limit your shape choice. And of course, another obvious variable might be the size of items you intend to stow. A 10-foot extension ladder or kayak cannot fit in an 8 x 8 foot shed.

This steep-roofed saltbox mimics aspects of a typical home, including decorative window trim, architectural asphalt shingles, and even a hint at a screen door.

▶ ROOFLINES

The design of the roof is one of the most important choices you will make as it will dictate the architectural style of the structure.

Consider the two issues: aesthetics and difficulty. While pyramid and mansard roof are certainly attractive, their construction is complex and there are many challenges when building them. A simple shed-style roof is by far the easiest to construct, but lacks the charm of a saltbox or the farm-and-barn ethic of a gambrel. A gable roof with a medium-to-strong pitch offers a great middle ground: classic lines, lots of headroom, and beginner-to-intermediate level difficulty.

Consider the other significant feature in your yard: your house. While your shed doesn't need to be a miniature copy of your house, selecting a roofline for your shed that mimics your home's can provide symmetry.

While looking at your house, take note of a couple of other basic features. Is the siding shingle, clapboard, barn board, or brick? What kind of windows do you have, double hung, sliders, casement? Do the doors have a specific style and are they wood or fiberglass? What size or style of trim is predominant? Use these features to guide the design of your shed.

This Dutch Colonial gambrel roof is a classic for barns.

ROOF STYLES

A roof does more than keep out the rain; it often defines the architectural style of your home. Below are the basic styles.

Shed. It's the simplest to build and has a modern, utilitarian feel.

Gable. Here's the classic Cape Cod look. Ranches have a shallower pitch. The saltbox roof is similar, with one wall higher than the other for more overhead space and the ridgeline off center.

Gambrel. Some folks call it Dutch Colonial. It's the standard for barns.

Hip. A strong roof with no gable siding to paint, but framing it is tricky.

Pyramid. It's the strongest, with triangles on every face. The building must be square.

Mansard. A popular Victorian style with European flavor. There's usable space in the rafters.

Take one last look at your conceptual floor plan. Where exactly did you place the door?

There are several different types of doors used on sheds, but the two most common are hinged and sliding. Hinged doors take up less space and close more tightly and securely. You can opt for a single-or double- hinged door, depending on the size of the structure and the size of the items that need to be moved in and out. Unlike your house, shed doors almost always open outward. Sliding doors are easier to install and glide completely out of the way but require additional wall space to slide over when opened.

The specifics of your shed's door placement are important. Doors are often placed on the gable or short end of the building, which looks attractive but can make it virtually impossible to reach items stored at the rear of the shed.

An alternative is to put the door on the long sidewall, so you'll be able to access items to the right, left, and back. If you live in a snowy climate, this can backfire as snow slides off the roof and lands directly in front of the door.

A third option is to install two doors, one on each gable-end wall, to allow you to easily reach items from either end of the shed.

Two doors can also be installed on adjacent gable-end and side walls, although this eliminates potential storage space opportunities along the inside where that second door sits.

Weigh these pros and cons carefully before making your final determination. Doors can either be bought new or purchased used from an architectural salvage facility or a non-profit material reuse center. You can also build a door from scratch, which will be covered in chapter 4.

Two doors makes for easy access, but less wall storage space.

▶ WINDOW PLACEMENT

Windows are not necessary in a shed. If you plan to use your shed for storage and only occasionally visit to fetch tools, a windowless structure may be the way to go. It's also the safest if you have any concerns about break-ins. Remember, unless you plan to bring electricity to the structure, your light will be limited to what enters through the open door, so you should keep a flashlight on a shelf just inside the entrance.

A window or two (or more) can brighten the interior of your shed, allowing you to change a spark plug on the mower or search for the right-sized socket wrench.

You can even close the door behind you to keep out the rain or cold. Gardeners may consider southerly windows that bring in enough sunlight to start seedlings. For non-gardeners, your window

placement will be driven by aesthetics.

As a rule of thumb, aesthetics suggest a search for balance. A single window will usually be centered. A wall with two windows should have them evenly spaced from the center, and of equal size. A wall with

Transom windows provide lots of light with minimal impact on storage capacity.

Using plexiglass or polycarbonate panels, your shed can double as a greenhouse.

Shutters and trim add attractive detail.

a door on the left will benefit from a window on the right. A door in the middle may demand two small windows, flanking it on either side.

Generally, windows in a shed are more about letting in light than about getting a view from inside, so they don't need to be large. In fact, smaller windows take up less precious space that might otherwise be used for shelving or wall-hanging storage. If you want to look out of them, place them at head height or a little below (4 to 6 feet high). If light is the priority, place windows high on a wall to illuminate the space while still allowing for a workbench with cabinets or shelves below. Transom windows work well for this reason.

Another possibility is to install skylights, or Plexiglass or translucent roof panels.

Shed windows generally don't need to open, but if you do feel strongly about ventilation and letting the summer breeze rustle through, sliding, single- or double-hung windows are all options. A cheaper and simpler option is to use a fixed window and add a couple of hinges so it can swing open. (See chapter 4.)

SHED NATION CITIZEN

 I designed this poolhouse to cover the pool pump and filter, to store the lawn tractor, and to serve as a party area. In the spring, it doubles as a greenhouse. I use the upper area for storage—it has attic-style stairs that pull down with a rope. The exterior is standard 2 x 4 wall construction with pine and 4 x 8 sheets of cedar with 3-inch grooves. First I assembled the walls. Next, I did the rafter layout on the driveway, and my wife helped me hoist them up on top of the walls. The plywood roof is covered with tar paper and asphalt shingles. This project took about six weekends to build.
—*JACK REHDER, St. Louis, MO*

Materials

You'll have lots of decisions to make while building your shed, but two choices will dramatically affect the look of the building: the materials you choose for your siding and for your roof. And they are choices you will need to live with for a long time.

▶ SIDING

→ **SOLID WOOD.** For siding, the first choice for most shed builders is solid wood, in beveled clapboards, shingles, shakes, or shiplap barn board. These products are typically made from red or white cedar, but they are also available in pine, spruce, redwood, cypress and Douglas fir. Solid wood is the standard and is unmatched for beauty and durability. It takes a wide variety of finishes well, offers some insulation value (which is not as critical in a shed as in a house), is easy to repair and install, and is available pre-stained, primed or unfinished in many styles.

Solid wood siding is arguably the best choice for the environment as well. It's a renewable resource that doesn't emit many pollutants during its manufacture, and at the end of its life, it is biodegradable provided it hasn't been treated with a preservative.

The downside is that wood must be painted or stained to prevent degradation by the sun's ultraviolet rays and by water, and then maintained with fresh coats of paint or stain every few years. But for a shed-sized structure, this periodic maintenance can be quick, inexpensive, and painless.

→ **COMPOSITE WOOD.** A relatively inexpensive variation on the wood theme is composite wood including plywood sheet materials, a grooved version of which (called Texture-111) mimics the look of vertical barnboard. OSB (Oriented Strand Board) and hardboard products are finely processed wood fibers bonded under heat and pressure. The T-111 ("tee-one-eleven") generally comes in 4 x 8 sheets, so it can be installed quickly. The OSB and hardboard can be in sheets or molded to look like clapboards, though no matter how hard the manufacturers try, they can never really make composite look like solid wood.

And due to their composite nature and the use of adhesives and preservatives, they are not biodegradable products. Hardboard siding failed on hundreds of holes in the '80s and '90s, but today's hardboard siding is quite different: added preservatives, primers, and adhesives.

→ **MASONRY.** An alternative is fiber-cement, a composite of Portland cement, sand, and cellulose fibers. It can be purchased in beveled planks, shingles or in 4 x 8 foot sheets. It's easy to apply, though beware breathing the silica dust created during the cutting of the boards. Termite- and fireproof, fiber-cement siding carries long warranties (coverage for 50 years is common) and is a good choice in hot and humid climates because it prohibits fungus growth. It does, however, require regular topcoat maintenance.

→ **VINYL.** Vinyl and metal siding, which flourished during the 1970s through 1990s were seen as godsends because of their indefinite lifespan and low-maintenance appeal, though vinyl has lost some of that luster due to growing environmental awareness. It is made from polyvinyl chloride (PVC), the same stuff that serves so ably in plumbing drain lines. PVC production has been blamed for high rates of cancer and other illness in the workers who produce it, and arguably, for people living near production facilities. Vinyl is built to last and will do so on your shed as well as lasting forever in the landfill when finally disposed there.

Texture-III plywood

Cedar Shakes

Cedar Shingles

Cedar Clapboard

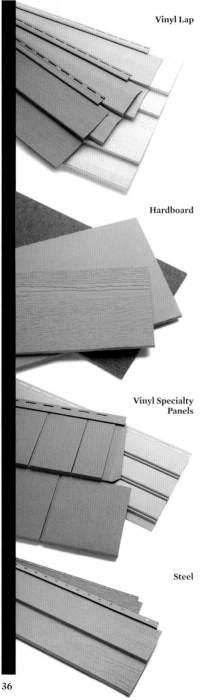

Vinyl Lap

Hardboard

Vinyl Specialty Panels

Steel

Vinyl's biggest selling point is that it's low maintenance. It can be washed clean with a garden hose and it never needs painting or staining. On the downside, vinyl products offer fewer color choices than painted or stained wood, and though better grades (.042 inches, or more) are rugged, they can still be damaged by impact (from an errant baseball, for instance), severe wind, heat from a nearby barbecue grill, or even the sun reflecting off a window. Finding replacement components can sometimes prove difficult or impossible, especially if the manufacturer is no longer in business.

New product offerings and features such as wood-like textures, shingle- and shake-style panels, more appealing trim components, and deeper colors have all improved the look of vinyl, but beware that the deeper colors will absorb more heat, which can, in turn, cause expansion and leave the siding looking wavy or rippled.

→ **METAL.** Metal siding, usually aluminum or steel, is a step up from vinyl in durability, but it has many of the same limitations and a few additional ones. Metal siding comes in limited colors, is subject to denting, and is difficult for the homeowner to install and repair. On the other hand, metal siding dents are easier to repair than the holes and cracks that plague vinyl, and metal products are fireproof. The material and installation costs of aluminum are less expensive than steel, but both cost more than vinyl. And metal can be recycled at the end of its lifespan.

SIDING COST COMPARISON

Materials costs do fluctuate over time and from place to place, but for the sake of comparison, here are some costs for typical siding options by the 10 × 10 foot square, not including installation, as of mid-2009.

- T-111 panels are about the cheapest way to go at about $100 per square.
- Vinyl siding panels are relatively inexpensive at about $250 per square, but may require professional installation, depending on your capabilities.
- Fiber-cement siding costs closer to $400, while aluminum siding is about $450-$500, and might also need a professional for installation.
- Pine clapboard or bevel siding costs about $500 per square, with cedar clapboards slightly more.
- Cedar shingles and shakes can cost as much as $700.

▶ ROOFING

Roofs are extremely tough environments for any material. In temperate climates, roof temperatures easily range from 120º F in the summer to well below freezing in the winter. Snow, ice, rain, and hail pound away season after season. And sunlight's harmful UV radiation is a constant throughout the year. There are many roofing options available. What's right for you depends on your taste, your budget, and the durability you desire.

→ **ASPHALT SHINGLES.** The most commonly used roofing material in the United States is the asphalt shingle. They are made by pressing mineral granules into an asphalt-saturated cellulose-fiber or fiberglass mat. There are different variations, including strip shingles, laminated shingles, interlocking shingles and oversize shingles, with three or four tabs, or none at all. Depending on the variety and quality you choose, you will get shingles rated to last between 15 and 30 years, and able to withstand winds of between 60 and 110 mph.

Asphalt shingles are generally the cheapest roofing option when considering cost per year of service, and they are fairly easy to install. But they are a petroleum-based product and are virtually impossible to recycle, which puts them low on the list for people searching for environmentally-friendly building materials.

Cedar Shingles and Shakes

Spanish Tile

Standing-Seam Metal

→ **WOOD SHINGLES.** Wood shingles and shakes, generally made from cedar, come in a variety of sizes and styles. These require specific installation methods, such as skip sheathing (leaving space of several inches to allow for air circulation beneath and between the long boards that the shingles are nailed to), and are more difficult to install than asphalt. But they look great, so much so that many other roofing products try to imitate them. The shingles have smooth surfaces and square edges, while the shakes are split instead of cut. This yields a rough surface and irregular edges. Wood shingles are long-lasting—up to 40 years—and are made from a renewable resource.

Unfortunately, wood is expensive—typically three times the cost of premium asphalt. It also requires periodic treatment with preservatives to keep the wood from drying out, warping, and cracking. And wood can be susceptible to discoloration, mildew, fungus, and rot, especially in a shady spot and a damp climate.

→ **METAL.** Metal roofing, usually of steel, aluminum, or copper, is available in several forms. Vertically installed steel or aluminum panels, joined together edge to edge on-site, is called standing-seam roofing. Also available are ribbed panels that have lapped joints on the ends. These products look crisp, and are popular on the steep roofs of snow country where the snow will slide off them easily. They are low-maintenance, impact and wind-resistant, and durable and have a life expectancy of up to 50 years, depending on the product. And they come pre-finished in a large variety of colors.

Copper roofs make a visually bold statement. They are not pre-finished, and they weather naturally from new-penny bright to a soft green patina (though the acidic rain that falls in the northeastern U.S. can turn it more to dark brown or black). Both steel and copper are a higher-cost option than asphalt (as much as two to four times more), but the longer lifespan may offset that. Additionally, standing-seam roofs require a degree of expertise to install correctly, so you may need to factor in the cost of professional installation. Metal panels are more DIY-friendly.

Environmentally, metal roofs have pros and cons. A lot of energy and pollutants are generated making them. However, up to 25 percent of the steel used in their manufacture is recycled from scrapped automobiles. Their long lifespan means they are infrequently replaced, and when they are, they can usually be recycled again.

→ **TILE.** If you live in the southwestern US or another area where tile is prevalent, you might consider this as an option. Tile is a beautiful material that has proven itself over hundreds of years and is the preferred roofing product in many European countries. Mission-style clay tiles have a half-round shape that is slightly tapered so that one course neatly fits under the next. Ceramic roof tiles are available in many colors and shapes, including slate- and shake-like products. Tiles cast from integrally colored concrete are a lower-cost alternative to clay and ceramic.

Advantages of tile include durability (you can expect 50 years or more of service); superior resistance to UV rays, wind, and fire; low maintenance; and easy repair, assuming you have the foresight to store a few spare tiles. Disadvantages include breakage from impact (for example, from a fallen tree branch), their heavy weight,

and high initial price. A tile roof will cost between two and three times more than a premium asphalt roof and potentially even more if the tile is not available locally and must be shipped.

→ **SLATE.** Slate is another good-looking roofing product, popular in regions where it's quarried, but less so otherwise due to shipping costs. Like tile, it is extremely durable and resistant to fire and wind damage, but it's even more expensive. As a completely natural material, it ranks high for environmental green-ness. Installation can be done by non-professionals, but requires a degree of care and patience, with each tile requiring the pre-drilling of holes to prevent breakage while fastening.

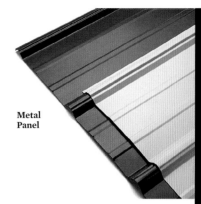

Metal Panel

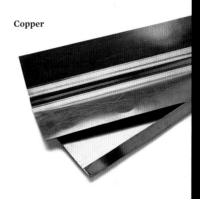

Copper

Stamped Metal

ROOFING MATERIAL COSTS

While materials costs fluctuate, here are some costs for roofing options by the 10 × 10 foot square, as of mid-2009.

- Asphalt shingles provide the most bang for your buck, costing between $40 and $55 per square for three-tab shingles and $50 to $80 for architectural shingles.
- Wood shingles and shakes are almost triple the price of asphalt, running in the $150-$200 range, but they can last longer.
- Metal roofs vary in price, depending on the material (aluminum or steel) and the format. Metal sheet panels cost about $100 per square, while standing seam roof systems jump to $400 to $500 per square, plus installation if you need to hire out.
- Clay tile and slate roofing materials, depending on whether they are readily available in your area, can cost between $400 and $800 per square, with slate at the upper end of that range.

Drawing It Up

Armed as you now are with a sense of your shed's size, purpose, location, architectural style, and the key materials you might use, it is time to flesh out your vision on paper.

Even if you are not artistically inclined, you do have the ability to draw up your prospective shed. Pull out your graph paper, pencil, and a ruler or straight edge. You will need four rectangles, one for each exterior wall. These are called "elevations," and will provide a view looking directly at the structure from straight on. You'll use the same measuring system you used for the shed size (floor plan) exercise you did earlier: ½ inch = 1 foot. Start by drawing your 8- or 12- or 22-foot wall length.

Next, you must determine the height of the walls. Your door placement will play a critical role. Let's assume you are drawing up a shed with a gable roof. You know that you must fit through the door, preferably without whacking your head each time, so it should be at least a couple of inches taller than you are (or the tallest person who will regularly be using it). Standard doors are 6'8", but it doesn't necessarily have to be this height, especially if you plan to build the door yourself. If your door is on the gable (or peak) end, then you have plenty of height to work with, but if it's on the long wall, with the roof sloping down over it, you might be more

restricted. Fill in your elevations with any windows you intend to include. Try them at different sizes and locations.

Remember to consider your purpose: Are you looking for light, ventilation, a view? How do you meet that goal without sacrificing valuable storage space?

For your elevations, your gable end walls will be formed by a rectangle topped by a triangle. The triangle's height will be a representation of your roof pitch. Roof pitches are commonly delineated by the number of inches the roof rises over the course of each horizontal foot. If the roof rises 8 inches every 12 horizontal inches, then it is said to be an 8 in 12 roof. If the roof rises more steeply, say 12 inches every foot, it's a 12 in 12 roof (which also happens to have a 90° angle at the peak). Roofs are only rarely steeper than 12 in 12 (think Gothic). Your roof pitch will depend on what looks good to you, how much headroom or overhead storage you might seek, height restrictions (if any) your municipality might have placed on you, and your

(right) This utilitarian shed has a hinged door on the long wall, providing accessibility to stored items.

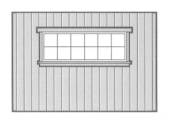

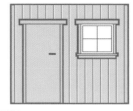

VERTICAL SIDING

Sketches provide the opportunity to explore the potential look of your shed, including siding materials and textures, and window and door placement. (bottom) Add roofs to your elevations, trying out different styles and materials.

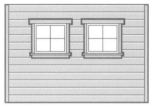

HORIZONTAL SIDING

geographical location (pitches vary with climate).

If you're going with a gable roofline, draw isosceles triangles resting atop the two end wall rectangles. (Isosceles means the two angles in the bottom corners are equal.) Play around with the height of the peak, adjusting it up or down to try out different roof pitches. If you favor the simplicity of a shed-style roof, you'll draw a right triangle, continuing your wall straight up on one side and then dropping the hypotenuse (the long side, opposite the right angle) back down to the top edge of the opposite wall.

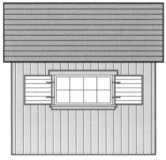

GABLE

For a saltbox, you'll take the center peak of an isosceles triangle and move it left or right, prompting an asymmetry between the two base angles and between the two legs dropping from the peak. The further you push the peak left or right, the greater the asymmetry.

For a gambrel roof, start with an isosceles triangle and then use each leg as the base of a second triangle, this one bulging out from the peak before dropping sharply to the wall top. In effect, a gambrel has two slopes of gable on each side, one steeper than 12 in 12, and one less steep.

Once you've played around with a few different roof styles and pitches and honed in on one,

GAMBREL

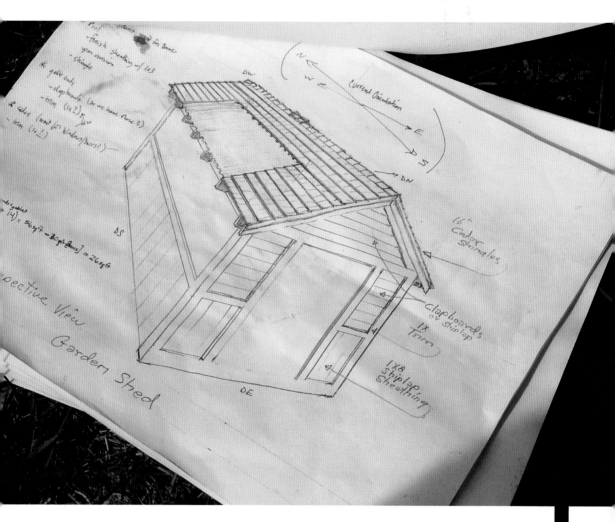

extend the eaves down by 4 to 8 inches, and then go to your long walls and add rectangles that will become the front and back roof. Your roof rectangles can be a little wider than the wall below, providing an overhang on each end of the structure known as a rake.

Now start adding and working with your details. If things feel cramped or too barren, add or subtract, lengthen or shorten, grow or shrink doors, windows, or wall heights until things feel right. Finally, add details like window and corner trim, roofing and siding materials, door and window styles, even shutters, window boxes, door hinges and latches, and any other decorative touches you are considering. Sketch in your roofing and siding materials with some horizontal or vertical lines to represent the

Consider trying a three-dimensional perspective drawing to help lift your shed off the plane of the page.

clapboards, asphalt shingles, or barnboard.

Later on, you'll redraw your plan with the skin peeled off, revealing the framing that will happen underneath. But for the time being, this rough plan is enough to get you started.

DIY or Ready-Made?

Once you've settled on the basic size, shape, and look of the shed of your dreams, ask yourself this important question: Exactly how much construction are you prepared to do?

If you have limited building skills or spare time, there are several options. You can go the simplest route and order a ready-made shed from a local supplier or home center, which can be delivered intact to your property.

If your shed needs are simple, you can consider purchasing a kit. The least expensive kits (which can come in a variety of designs, from Colonial gable sheds to storybook cottages) come with pre-cut parts, hardware, and a building plan. For a little more money, you'll get a kit that is partially assembled (or panelized) with installed siding, a pre-shingled roof, and pre-hung doors and windows. No matter what kind of kit you buy, the job of assembly will be easier if the manufacturer provides not only a plan with written assembly instructions, but also a DVD or video of the process, along with online or telephone support.

If your carpentry and framing skills are up to the task, or if you are looking for a dynamic learning experience, a purchased, professionally-designed plan dramatically simplifies the design process— and allows you to make choices about the quality of the lumber and other materials you use as your budget will allow. Plus you can modify the design. Taking this route gives you support on the design end, but still allows you to build it yourself.

If you're a purist and want to tackle it all, the rewards are well worth it. You have the opportunity to create a unique structure that meets both your needs and tastes. You'll also have the incredible opportunity to learn about carpentry, tools, and materials, gain the satisfaction of doing it yourself, and likely save money in the process.

No matter the path you decide to take, the following chapters will provide the details, descriptions, and definitions you'll need on your journey for the perfect shed.

If you don't mind losing some control of your project's design, detailed building plans are available for a reasonable fee for virtually any design.

Foundation
and
Floors

The foundation of your shed provides the basis for a solid, long-lasting, functional structure.

CHAPTER 2

Foundations

Depending on the size of the structure you intend to build, and your climate and building codes, you may need to excavate and create a frost-proof foundation, or you may be able to simply create an on-grade foundation.

THE RIGHT TOOLS
FOR THE JOB

Here's a list of the "must-have" tools, whether you are building a shed or a house:

- Framing hammer
- Hand-held circular saw
- Hand saw
- Table saw
- Jig saw or scroll saw
- Levels of assorted lengths (9-, 24-, and 48-inch, at a minimum)
- Tape measure (25- or 30-foot, with locking device)
- Tool belt
- Chalk line reel
- Cordless and corded drill
- Carpenters pencils
- Utility knife (retractable)
- Framing square
- Speed Square
- Cat's paw (nail puller)
- Extension Cords
- Ladders (6-foot and 8-foot)

Sheds typically those more than 200 square feet in size—and some smaller structures with electricity, plumbing, or insulation—typically require permanent foundations that extend down below the frost line. These are constructed of poured-concrete piers or buried wooden posts resting on a concrete footing. Your local building department will provide specific code requirements and frost-line depth in your area. Smaller structures, including most garden and storage sheds—even in extremely cold climates—don't require a frost-proof foundation, which means it's not necessary to excavate down three, four, or five feet into the ground to get below the designated frost-line in your climate.

For the average small, unimproved garden shed, the simpler and less expensive on-grade version of a foundation is perfectly adequate. While the shed might shift a little with a winter frost heave, it will simply settle back into place come the spring thaw with no damage to the structure.

On-Grade Foundations

If you are using an on-grade foundation, you still have a few options to consider. Most wooden sheds are set on either concrete blocks or treated-lumber skids. Which option is right for you?

▶ SKID FOUNDATION

A skid foundation is probably the easiest to construct. Building on skids means that your shed is a non-permanent structure and can be moved. This fact can also relieve you of any property tax assessment that home improvements, additions, and new structures can trigger. Its non-permanent status may also simplify or help you get around challenging zoning restrictions.

A portable shed may also prove useful to you if you are using it to house animals, such as chickens, and want to rotate their pecking grounds periodically. Or perhaps your structure is a kids' playhouse, and it needs to move further and further from the house as the kids get older (and louder). Or perhaps the skids will be for show, and you'll never move the structure an inch.

A skid foundation comprises treated timbers running parallel on opposite sides for the length of the structure, each on a bed of tamped-down gravel 4 to 6 inches deep. The gravel will act as a stabilizer, allowing ground water to drain away without erosion or mud-induced destabilization. The building's floor frame is then constructed on or between these skids. The skids themselves should be at least four inches wide and 6 to 8 inches tall, so they provide a stable enough base and enough ground clearance to keep the floor decking away from ground water. Using six-by-sixes or eight-by-eights is probably the most common and straightforward method, though you could

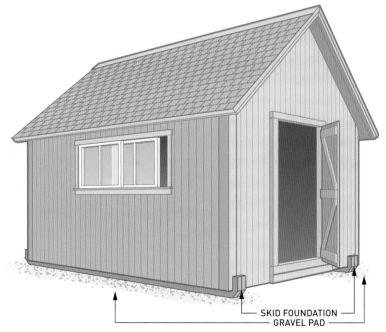

SKID FOUNDATION
GRAVEL PAD

Skids resting on flat stones, blocks or gravel are a simple foundation method. The deck can be built either on top of the skids, or between them.

fabricate them by nailing together three two-by-sixes or two-by-eights (a wood sandwich).

They should be placed no further than 8 feet apart, or they may not provide enough support for the center of the floor deck. It's not necessary for them to be flush with the outside of the structure; they can sit 6 to 12 inches in and under the deck, but you probably don't want to push in much more than that or the cantilevered sides of the shed may become too springy.

Bringing them in a bit also serves to hide them from view, and can simplify the detail of how and where to cut the bottom of your siding later.

If you do intend to move the shed periodically, cut off the lower corner of each skid at a 45° angle so that it will slide more easily, without digging into and mutilating the ground as soon as you pull it with your truck or tractor.

Make certain to use pressure-treated lumber rated for "ground contact" any time wood will be directly touching earth. Pressure-treated wood is chemically treated to resist rot and decay.

It is critical that the ground on which the skids will sit is level, so if your site has a slope to it, you will need to remove material from the higher area. Never attempt to build up a lower section with dirt or gravel because it will likely erode away, leaving you with your very own Leaning Tower of Pisa.

▶ CONCRETE BLOCK FOUNDATION

A full-footprint gravel bed is ideal, though not critical.

Another oft-used foundation strategy is the concrete block method. This type of foundation is straightforward and inexpensive. The blocks are laid in straight rows, at consistent intervals running the length of your shed's footprint. How many rows of blocks you will need, and the number of blocks per row, depends on the size of your shed. For a 6- or 8-foot-wide shed, two rows of blocks—each positioned to directly support one of the long walls—should suffice. For a wider shed, a third row should be placed midway between, or your floor might end up with a sag. Space the blocks in each row evenly, one every 4 to 6 feet.

Start by laying out and staking the four corners of the shed. With a helper, measure the distance from front left to the back right corner, and compare that to

(left) Use a straight two by four to help check that your foundation blocks are level.

the distance between the other two corners. Non-identical measurements means you are out of "square" and need to tweak your stake placement until you get it right. Once you do, run a string around the perimeter, from corner to corner. This is your shed's footprint.

As with the skid method, concrete blocks also require a degree of excavation. The most diligent option is to clear sod and soil to a depth of 6 inches for the entire footprint of the shed, and then pour and tamp (compact) a 4-inch gravel bed throughout.

A less diligent but perfectly adequate method is to dig 6-inch-deep depressions in each corner and every other location where you intend to lay a block. Then lay a 4-inch-deep gravel bed in each hole and tamp it down. The rationale in either case is that the gravel will act as a stabilizer and aid in drainage.

Place the blocks (which generally measure 4 × 8 × 16 inches) on the gravel pads and make sure they are level. Make sure to use solid blocks rather than hollow ones, which have a tendency to crack.

Working on a level site is optimal, but if your site is gently sloped, set and level the blocks on the uphill side first, leaving 4 to 6 inches above grade, then use a 4-foot level taped to a long, straight two-by-four to determine the height of the downhill blocks.

You can make up the difference in grade by stacking blocks, either two or three 4-inch-thick blocks,

(top) Assorted shims can be used to offset minor height variations. (middle right) A compacted gravel pad beneath each block provides a solid, level base. (middle left) Construction adhesive will help keep stacked blocks from kicking out.

or a 4-incher capped by a 2-inch-thick patio block.

If you need to stack more than a foot to gain the height you need, it is advisable to excavate the high end of the structure instead, as you begin to run the risk of the stack toppling over or kicking out during normal ground heaving or settling. Use construction adhesive between any blocks you do stack to minimize the possibility of slippage or sliding while building the floor deck and structure above.

Ensure each block is individually level, and check and double-check that your block tops are level with one another by using your 4-foot level taped to the straight two-by-four. If you find minor height variations, you can use wood blocks, cedar shims, or even strips of asphalt shingle to offset the difference.

SHED NATION CITIZEN

Two winters ago my old metal shed collapsed when the roof caved in from snow. I really enjoy doing some sweating and building things at my own pace, so I designed a new, sturdier shed modeled after a log cabin. I just like the rustic look of log construction. I used 160 landscape ties, each one 8 feet long by 3 inches thick by 5 inches wide. The ties are held together with construction adhesive and 3-inch countersunk screws. I coated the outside of the shed with deck sealer to waterproof it. The sealer also darkened the ties, giving the shed a nicely aged appearance.

The roof is made of Ondura, an asphalt-impregnated corrugated roofing. I chose red Ondura because it's reminiscent of old-fashioned "tin" roofs. The roofing is supported by a ¾-inch plywood deck. Inside the shed is open, with no posts. I built a loft under the highest portion of the roof by screwing two logs to the inside walls, one on each side. On top of those logs I framed out a two-by-four floor topped with one-by-four planking.

The shed has six framed windows, some made from ¼-inch tempered glass that I salvaged from old vending machines. It took two months to build. I liked the shed so much that I built a second, smaller one last year.

—RICHARD A. DEBRASKY, PA

Frost-Proof Foundations

For larger structures in need of a more permanent foundation, you may need to excavate down below the frost line and pour concrete footings. If you've never worked with concrete before, this may sound intimidating and overwhelming. The good news is that it's really far less complicated than you'd anticipate.

▶ POURED-CONCRETE PIERS

The most challenging aspect is making sure to pour your piers in the right location. First, using your staked footprint, mark on the ground where your holes need to be dug. Beside the four corners, you'll need foundational support ideally every six to eight feet.

You can mark your spots with anything from spray paint to flour, but don't just make a little 6-inch "X" on the ground, as it will be removed with your first shovelful or backhoe scoop, and then it's anybody's guess where your spot might have been. Rather, make your "X," and then extend each leg out 2 to 3 feet from the center. Next, connect the outer ends of each leg so you end up with a circle 4 to 6 feet in diameter, centered on the "X." You can also make three or four progressively smaller concentric circles, creating a target. As you dig away, your hole will get deeper and wider, but your target circles will keep you centered. Your hole will need to be about 2 feet in diameter at the bottom. How deep you go is dependent on the frost line in your area (anywhere from 2 to 6 feet). If you skimp on the depth you may find that pier heaved out at a 15° angle next spring.

Take care to keep the Sonotube plumb while backfilling the hole.

1/2" THREADED "J" BOLT

"SONOTUBE" WAXED CARDBOARD CONCRETE FORM

"BIG FOOT" PLASTIC FOOTING FORM

8" MIN

BELOW FROST LINE

1/2" REBAR

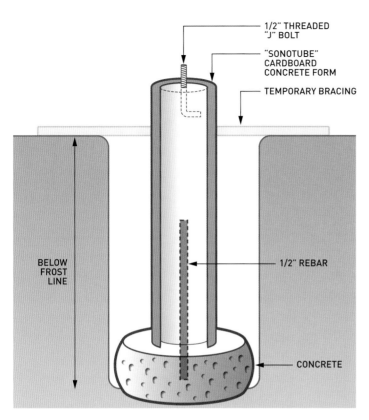

1/2" THREADED "J" BOLT

"SONOTUBE" CARDBOARD CONCRETE FORM

TEMPORARY BRACING

BELOW FROST LINE

1/2" REBAR

CONCRETE

A Bigfoot allows the footer and pier to be poured simultaneously.

Once your holes are dug, pour a concrete footing in each. The easiest method is to simply fill the bottom of your hole with 8 to 10 inches of concrete. As it begins to cure, drive a 2- to 3-foot length of ½-inch rebar into the center of the footer. This will strengthen the joint between the footer and the pier. Then lower a Sonotube fiber-form tube (precut to the height of your hole plus six inches of reveal) right down onto the top of the footing, surrounding the rebar.

In a perpendicular alignment, screw two pieces of scrap lumber, each long enough to straddle your hole, to the tube at ground level to act as bracing. When you've got all four corners set, get your tape measure and your level and spend some time determining that you've got your tubes in the exact right spots, that they are precisely vertical, and that they are cut to heights that are level with one another. When you are triply sure you've got all those elements aligned, carefully backfill the holes around the tubes making certain to not jostle them out of plumb,

and then mix the concrete in a wheelbarrow or concrete mixer and fill the tubes with the concrete right to the brim, leveling the top with a piece of scrap wood.

An acceptable footing variation is to use a plastic, conical base manufactured by Bigfoot Systems, with a telescoping opening on top of which various diameter Sonotubes will snugly fit. With the Bigfoot, you'll attach the Sonotube first, and then mix and pour your concrete straight down the tube and into the footing, filling both in one fell swoop. The smallest size Bigfoot (20-inch diameter) should be sufficient. Because the foot and tube act as one unit, you'll need to check for location and level before pouring any concrete. Insert a ½-inch rebar rod mid-way through the pour to tie together the Bigfoot and the Sonotube sections.

If you live in a hurricane-prone place, you may be required to sink a J-bolt into the footing before it cures. A J-bolt is a metal rod with a hook on one end and a thread on the other. Sink the hooked end down into the cement while it is still a liquid, with the threaded end rising about 2½ inches above the surface of the concrete at the center of the tube. Hold it in place until you are sure the concrete has solidified enough to not swallow it up. Later, you will drill a hole through the mudsill that will rest on the piling and affix it with the appropriate-sized nut.

A slightly easier and cheaper frost-proof option is to pour a simple footing on which a wood post rests. This methodology is most appropriate in dryer and warmer climates, so check with your local building department to see if it is acceptable in your area.

Though you still need to dig down to the frost line, in this situation, your hole only needs to be about 12 to 16 inches wide, potentially allowing the use of a post-hole digger rather than a shovel or heavy machinery. Fill the bottom of your hole with about a foot of concrete and let it cure. Then drop a pressure-treated six-by-six down onto the center of the footing and carefully backfill the hole with a mixture of crushed stone and sand to about 6 inches below grade, making sure to keep your post perfectly vertical. Tamp the backfill. Then cut a piece of 2-inch-thick rigid foam as large as you can go and still fit in your post hole. Cut a hole in the middle (making a donut) to the size of your post, and slide the foam down the post to the backfill material. This will help contain any frost action down below. Then backfill the rest of the hole to ground level. Make an effort to steer excess groundwater away from these posts by creating small swales or drainage ditches. Many people would associate this footing and post method with a pole barn framing strategy, but with some minor tweaks, you'll be able to utilize it for typical stick-framing just as easily.

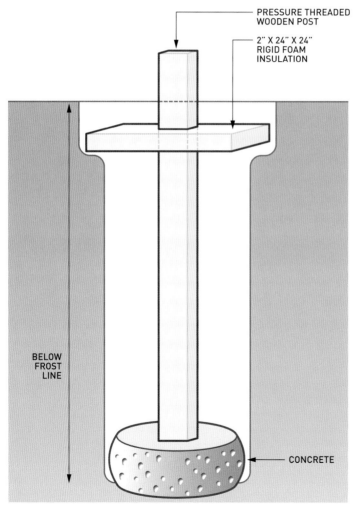

PRESSURE THREADED WOODEN POST

2" X 24" X 24" RIGID FOAM INSULATION

BELOW FROST LINE

CONCRETE

A pressure-treated post can rest directly on a concrete footer with the help of the right backfill and some insulation to protect against freezing.

▶ POURED-CONCRETE SLAB

A rented concrete mixer will allow faster, more efficient mixing.

One final option should be noted: pouring a concrete slab or pad. If integrated with a frost-proof foundation, this is the most complicated and expensive option, though it's worth considering in certain situations and for certain uses. For instance, if you intend to use the structure for any type of animal care or housing, such as for dogs or horses, or if you intend to store heavy equipment or vehicles, a concrete slab is unparalleled for strength and cleaning ease. But the deeper you need to dig into

the ground for the foundation, the deeper you will also need to dig into your wallet. However, if frost is not an issue in your locale at all, you might get away with a floating, or on-grade slab, which requires only 4 or 6 inches of concrete on a bed of gravel.

In either instance, and especially if you are pouring a frost-proof foundation, the DIYer should consider hiring out this portion of the job to a professional. The complexity of the task and permanence of the product calls for a degree

of know-how. Even for just the floating slab, you're likely be left with, at best, an imperfect finish, and at worst, a reason to bring in jackhammers to blast your handiwork to bits. But if you insist on doing it yourself, here are the basics for pouring a simple slab.

Concrete consists of cement and an aggregate of fine sand and gravel or crushed stone. When these dry ingredients are mixed with water, they create a chemical reaction with the cement that prompts

You will require many bags of dry-mix concrete for your shed's foundations.

the aggregate to bind into a dense, hard material. The initial hardening happens within just a few hours, depending on the percentage of water content. During this timeframe, the mason needs to work efficiently, before the mix hardens enough to become unworkable. The hardening (and real strengthening) continues for approximately four weeks, as long as moisture is still present within the concrete.

Though you can buy cement, sand, and gravel or crushed stone individually, for the sake of simplicity, purchase bags of dry-mix concrete. It comes pre-mixed to the appropriate proportions. A wheelbarrow will let you mix small batches; simply add water from a garden hose to the dry materials until they reach the appropriate consistency, and mix thoroughly with a shovel. But beware: even a small, 100-square-foot shed can require 1¼ cubic yards of concrete, enough to fill 30 or 40 wheelbarrows. Moving too slowly can mean your first batches may already be unworkable by the time you pour the last batch. A rented concrete mixer will allow faster, more efficient mixing, or you can order from a concrete company. But keep in mind, a concrete truck's delivery chute can only reach so far, so if your shed site is distant from the truck's access point, you will need to quickly and efficiently shuttle the concrete across the yard to your site via wheelbarrow.

To determine the amount of concrete you will need, multiply your slab length by width by thickness (in feet). A shed slab should be 3–4 inches thick. Then divide by 27 to get your cubic yards.

To install the pad, first excavate the site down about 6 inches. Use 2x lumber as formwork. The form must be as wide as the finished depth of concrete. Lay the subbase of gravel or crushed stone to a depth of 3 inches. Level the surface and compact it with a tamper made from a foot-square plywood pad screwed to a two-by-four or four-by-four handle.

Using string lines as a guide, erect the form using 2 × 2 inch wood stakes around the exterior to hold them in place. Prop them 3 inches up to allow for a subbase to be laid. Before nailing the planks to the stakes, check that the tops of the boards are level all the way around. If not, shim them.

Mix the concrete as near to the site as possible and lay a wood plank runway to allow your wheelbarrow easy access to the site. Start filling from one end of the site, pushing the concrete firmly into the corners. Keep working quickly, adding additional loads of concrete until it stands about ¾ inch above the top of the form work. Rake it level, then tamp down the concrete with the edge of a thick plank (screed rail) that is long enough to reach across the forms. With a helper, move from one end to the other and then back again, compacting the concrete with blows from the plank every couple of inches. Then remove excess concrete, using the plank in a sawing motion. Fill any low spots, then compact and level the concrete once more.

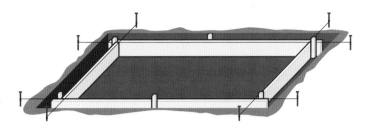

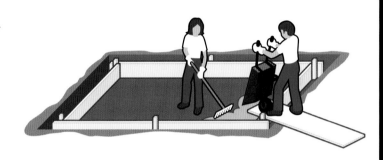

For a smoother finish, use a magnesium bull float, which is a form of trowel attached to a long handle. The trick is to keep the leading edge of the float inclined and off the surface of the slab as you push and pull it by manipulating the handle.

When you've got the desired degree of smoothness, cover the pad with sheets of plastic weighted down outside the perimeter of the forms with bricks or stones. This will help retain moisture during the curing process, providing a stronger end result. You can walk on the concrete in about three days, but wait about a week before removing the forms and erecting your shed.

Building the Deck

Once your foundation is in place and cured (if you've poured concrete), you are now ready to build the deck.

▶ CONCRETE BLOCKS OR CONCRETE PIERS

If you are building your shed on skids skip ahead to page 66. The deck, or floor, of the shed is a fairly straightforward project. It is comprised a mudsill and band joist perimeter, a center mudsill (if you have a central row of foundation blocks or piers), a series of floor joists running from side to side, and decking or flooring material.

First, cut your mudsills to length. Mudsills are 2 × 6 pieces of pressure-treated lumber that lay flat atop the foundation blocks, piers, or skids. The sills running along the long walls should run their full length and

lay flush to the outside edge of your blocks or piers. Short wall sills should be sandwiched between the side sills. Then cut 2 × 6 pressure-treated band joists to sit upright on top of the sill flush with the outer edge. Stagger the sills and band joists so they overlap at the corners. Nail each sill and joist combo together individually using 16d galvanized nails, before joining them to the adjacent segments. This will allow you to flip each unit to nail from underneath before it becomes too heavy and bulky to maneuver the whole floor frame.

Eliminating the front and back mud sills will save you a little bit of money and won't affect the strength of your deck, but it will reduce some of rigidity of the front band joist, which may haunt you a bit if you've got steps or a ramp leaning up against it. In this case, you'll probably want to make that joist double thickness to stiffen it up.

If you're working atop poured piers with anchors, you'll need to drill holes in the sills to

accommodate the threaded rod ends. Rather than laboriously measuring the spot where you need to drill, just put the sill in its proper position, but resting atop the threaded rod, and whack it hard several times with a hammer directly over each pier. Then flip the board over, look for the indentations the rod ends left behind, and drill away.

If you have a center foundation row of blocks or piers, cut an additional 2 × 6 pressure-treated sill to length and put it in place. If you don't have a front and back sill, nail this central sill on each end into the front joist. If you do install front and back sills, you'll need to tie them to the mid-sill with a plywood gusset or a metal tie-plate.

Once you've got your sills and band joists conjoined and in place, you are ready to cut all the 2 × 6 floor joists to length and set them between the two band joists and on top of the mudsills. You'll want to space the joists 16 inches on-center (o.c.), which means the distance from the center of one joist's thickness to the center of

A NAIL PRIMER

BOX NAIL: A nail with a flat head and a shank more slender than a common nail of the same length.

BRAD: A small finishing nail.

CASING NAIL: A nail with a small conical head and a shank more slender than a common nail of the same length, typically used in finish work where the head may remain visible.

COMMON NAIL: A nail with a slender shank, a flat head, and a diamond point.

CONCRETE NAIL: A hardened-steel nail with a fluted or threaded shank and a diamond point, typically used to hammer into concrete or masonry. Also called a masonry nail.

CUT NAIL: A nail with a tapering rectangular shank and a blunt point; cut from a rolled sheet of iron or steel.

DOUBLE-HEADED NAIL: A nail used to build temporary structures, such as scaffolding and formwork, with a flange on its shank to prevent it from being driven all the way in and to provide room for pulling. Also called a form nail or scaffold nail.

DRIVE SCREW: A metal fastener with a helically threaded shank that can be driven with a hammer and removed with a screwdriver.

FINISHING NAIL: A nail with a slender shank and a small, barrel-shaped head, typically driven slightly below the surface and covered with putty.

FLOORING NAIL: A nail used to fasten floor boards,

with a small conical head, a mechanically deformed shank, and a blunt diamond point.

RING-SHANK NAIL: A nail with a series of concentric grooves on its shank for increased holding power.

ROOFING NAIL: A nail with a barbed, threaded, or cement-coated shank and a broad, flat head, used to fasten shingles.

WIRE NAIL: A nail made by cutting or shaping a piece of round or elliptical wire.

Getting a handle on nail types and sizes, and knowing which to use in each situation, can feel daunting, so here's a little help. Nails are generally sold in 1-, 5- and 50-pound boxes, or sometimes loose from a bin and weighed on a scale. A carpenters' nail arsenal is primarily composed of five nail types: common, spiral, box, finishing, and roofing nails. A common nail is for heavy framing; its extra-thick shank and a wide, thick head provide it with great strength. A spiral nail is also used for framing. The spiraling ridges along its shank prompt it to rotate slightly as it is driven in, giving it extra grip.

A box nail is a thinner version of the common nail, which makes it less likely to split wood, but more likely to bend. A finishing nail's small, dimpled head is designed to be driven flush, and then sunk below the surface with a nailset so that it

won't show. A roofing nail's extra-wide head gives it dynamic holding power. The roofing nail is generally galvanized (coated with zinc) to prevent corrosion and rusting.

Nails are identified by "penny" size, which is abbreviated as "d." This originally referred to the cost of 100 nails, but now is used to indicate a nail's length, from a 2d nail (about one inch long) to a 16d (three and a half inches), all the way up to a 60d (six inches).

4d	6d	8d	10d	12d	16d	20d
1½"	2"	2½"	3"	3¼"	3½"	4"
38mm	51mm	64mm	76mm	83mm	89mm	102mm

PENNY: The designated length of a nail, from twopenny to sixtypenny. Symbol: d

SHANK: The straight, narrow part of a nail or bolt, between the head and the point.

EIGHTPENNY NAIL: A nail 2½ inches (64 mm) long.

SIXTEENPENNY NAIL: A nail 3½ inches (89 mm) long.

A DECKING PRIMER

Floors are supported by framing members called joists. These sit in box sills resting on or anchored to the foundation. The box sills are made of sill plates or mud sills that lie flat on the foundation and band joists that sit on edge. In an insulated, conditioned structure, a sill seal between the sill and foundation acts as a moisture and air barrier. Building codes often require sills to be made of pressure-treated lumber or a decay-resistant species of wood.

Floor joists are deep in profile in order to resist bending when under load. If the joists are too light, the floor will deflect noticeably and bounce when walked on. Depending on spacing, length of span and wood species, joists will range from 2 × 6 up to 2 × 10 or 2 × 12 in homes with spans up to 16 or 18 feet. Wider structures need a center beam to break the span. Wood blocking or metal bridging is often added between the joists to further stiffen the floor. 4 × 8 sheets of plywood or OSB are glued and nailed on top of the joists.

the next joist's thickness should be 16 inches. Since two-by-fours are actually only 1½ inches thick, the center of each is ¾ inch from its edge, meaning the void between joists will be 14½ inches. Starting at the front (short wall) band joist, measure 15¼ inches from the outside edge and mark your spot along the top of one of the long walls. That will be where you place the leading edge of the second joist. By making this first measurement ¾ inch shy, you'll be making your life easier when you lay the decking material atop the joists later on.

From there, keep adding and marking 16-inch intervals all the way to the far end. Depending on your shed's dimensions, you may come to the back end and discover a 20-inch interval and consider skipping the last joist. Don't do it. Add the additional joist at 16 inches, even if your last interval will only be 3 inches. Better to be too beefy than not beefy enough. Repeat the process on the opposite side and then cut the number of joists you need to the appropriate length. At this point, you can likely leave the pressure-treated lumber

behind and just use regular spruce two-by-sixes.

Before dropping the joists into place, sight down each board along the thin edge. The natural grain in wood has a tendency to arch a piece of lumber slightly. If you peer down the board with one eye right at board level, you can get a sense of whether it arches (crowns) or drips. Place the crown edge up. If the crown or dip is extreme, use a different board.

When you have the joists in place, make sure they are flush with the top of the band joist wherever they abut (if not, do some temporary shimming), and then nail them through each band joist with three 16d galvanized nails. Finally, toenail them into the central band sill, if you've got one. Toenailing simply means nailing through the joist at an angle so the nail exits near the bottom corner of the joist and pierces the sill below. You'll do this twice, one nail angling down from each side of the sill to make an X, though be sure to space them horizontally from one another so they don't actually collide.

Yet another option is to do away with the mud sills completely, set the band joists directly on your foundation, and hang the floor joists from joist hangers at 16 inches o.c. A joist hanger is a stainless steel U-shaped bracket that nails to the band joist, providing a seat for the floor joist to sit. The floor joists are then secured to the hangers using 1½-inch joist hanger nails.

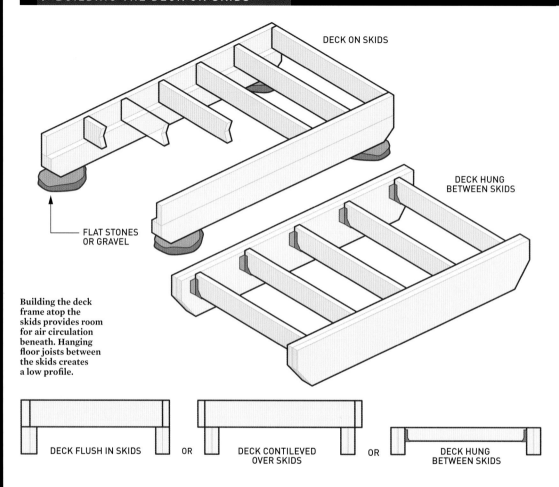

DECK ON SKIDS

DECK HUNG
BETWEEN SKIDS

FLAT STONES
OR GRAVEL

**Building the deck
frame atop the
skids provides room
for air circulation
beneath. Hanging
floor joists between
the skids creates
a low profile.**

DECK FLUSH IN SKIDS   OR   DECK CONTILEVED
OVER SKIDS   OR   DECK HUNG
BETWEEN SKIDS

Now let's rewind a bit for those who are building on skids. This is a simpler situation because you won't need to concentrate on the locations of concrete blocks or piers. You just assemble or cut the skids, lay them on the ground parallel to one another and the desired distance apart, and then build your deck within or on top of them.

The simplest method is to cut and hang your joists between the two skids, flush with their tops. You'll do this by measuring 16 inches o.c. along the length of the skids, and then utilizing joist hangers to affix them in place. Since your joist are two-by-sixes, the skids themselves will need to be at least 8 inches tall and likely taller to keep those

joists from hanging too close to the ground and sucking up moisture. Pressure-treated lumber might be appropriate for the joists in this case. Aside from the simplicity of this method, you also get a low-profile appearance.

In order to build the deck on top of the skids, just construct a band joist box (as described

on page 62). The joists will hang inside, either by sitting on a mudsill and nailing through the exterior of the box, or by utilizing joist hangers. You'll have a higher-profile building that will require a couple of steps or a ramp to get in and out. This additional height relieves the need for any pressure-treated lumber above the skids, and you'll also have a greater degree of air circulation beneath the structure, which reduces the potential for rot. Remember to put the crown edge facing up on your joists.

SHED NATION CITIZEN

I designed and built this storage barn for my lawn and garden equipment. The building measures 12 feet wide by 18 feet long. I partitioned off a 9 × 5 foot room for my wife, Maureen, to use as a potting shed for her gardening needs. There is an overhead storage area with folding stair access, as well as an exterior overhead door. It also has a workbench and electricity. It took about seven weeks, on and off, to build.
—EDWARD S. PRATT, Wells, VT

If you sank posts down to a footing, you'll need to cut the posts at the desired height (about six to twelve inches above the ground and level with one another) and build a girt around them. Using pressure-treated two-by-sixes, run two boards (sandwiching each post) from corner to corner along one long wall, flush with the tops of the posts. Midway between posts, add blocking between the boards to help stiffen them up. Repeat this process on the other long wall. This doubling up will provide extra strength for the floor joists and decking. Cap the short wall ends with more pressure-treated two-by-sixes, closing in the perimeter of the girt system. Then build a deck-framing box with regular two-by-sixes to rest atop these two girts.

Building a frame that straddles the posts provides extra strength for the joists and coming structure.

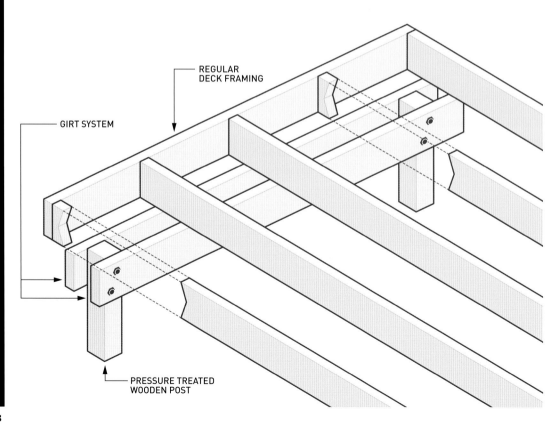

REGULAR
DECK FRAMING

GIRT SYSTEM

PRESSURE TREATED
WOODEN POST

Regardless of your foundation and deck framing methodology, the final step of applying decking is universal. Most people choose to use ¾-inch plywood because it is economical and has structural rigidity, but it is certainly possible to go with solid wood planks or tongue-and-groove (T&G).

Before applying any decking, if you are working on skids or concrete blocks it is imperative to check again for the squareness of your floor assembly. If you begin laying decking on an out-of-square base, you will quickly get frustrated by the fact that your decking edges cannot be made to sit flush with the band joists below. And once you have affixed some of your decking material, the chance to correct the situation disappears. So pull out your tape and compare diagonal measurements again between opposite corners.

If you come up with a disparity, use a rubber-headed sledgehammer (or regular sledgehammer with a piece of scrap wood covering your target to prevent aesthetic damage) and give the band joist some solid whacks in the corner that will correct the issue.

Once square, you're almost ready to begin laying your

decking. But first, if your deck assembly is simply resting on concrete blocks, your local building codes may require you to secure the floor frame with four steel-cabled ground anchors. Bolt one anchor to each corner of the frame and drive the hold-down spikes deep into the ground.

Staggered flooring provides greater stability.

For your shed floor, ¾-inch ACS plywood is the common choice, though some people opt for the T&G variety because the joints create a rigid floor that doesn't bounce or sag. Place your first sheet in the corner. You can double-check your frame's squareness by noting how closely the factory edges of the plywood follow the outer edge of the band joists. Since your joists are set at 16 inches o.c, your 8-foot-long piece of plywood should end smack in the middle of your sixth joist, with just enough meat to nail both the tail end of this first sheet, and the front end of the second. But, if things have gone awry and you've missed your mark, you'll need to cut back the sheet to the midway point of the nearest joist. Don't ever butt decking or sheathing in mid-air.

Once you're sure you've landed on the joist, nail the plywood down with 8d galvanized nails at 6- to 8-inch intervals. Then lay your next sheet abutting the first, and repeat the process until you reach the far end. If using T&G, hold a piece of scrap wood along the far end of the sheet and gently bang the sheet through the scrap with a sledge hammer to tap it into snug connectivity with the preceding sheet.

Stagger the next row by starting with a half-length piece of plywood. This helps with rigidity by eliminating four-corner intersections.

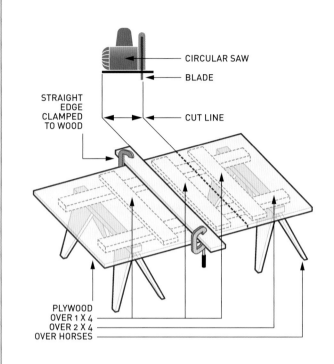

CIRCULAR SAW

BLADE

STRAIGHT EDGE CLAMPED TO WOOD

CUT LINE

PLYWOOD OVER 1 X 4 OVER 2 X 4 OVER HORSES

CUTTING STRAIGHT LINES

IN SHEET GOODS

No matter how skilled you are, and no matter how much meditation you practice, running a circular saw along a pencil or chalk line for a 4-or 8-foot length is bound to result in a curvy cut.

Here's a trade secret: For a 4-foot, width-wise cut, measure the distance from your saw blade to the edge of the saw's base plate. Then take your 4-foot level and clamp it to the plywood exactly that distance from your cut line. You've created a fence to guide your saw smoothly through the cut. For an 8-foot cut—unless you have an 8-foot level—cut a thin, 4- to 5-inch-wide strip from the edge of another piece of plywood and clamp that down to the board in question with the factory edge acting as your guide.

If opting for plank flooring instead of sheet goods, the concept is generally the same. You will want to use meaty 1½ or thicker T&G planks, though with certain strong species (Southern Yellow Pine, for instance) you

Ground anchors provide protection from hurricane force winds.

might be able to utilize 5/4-inch (1-inch-thick) boards. These will prove to be solid flooring, providing greater strength than even ¾-inch T&G plywood. Most people will opt for the widest planks they can find, preferably 6 inches and up, because they go on quicker and have a classic look. Run the installation across

the joists and stagger your rows as much as possible.

When you've got the last board cut and nailed down, hop up on the stage you've created for yourself and take a big bow. Congratulations! You've completed another major step in the process, and you are well on your way.

71

Building Stairs and Ramps

Unless you won't mind hopping onto and off of your deck for the rest of your life—sometimes with a kayak or a 50-pound bag of birdseed in your arms—you need to create a transition from ground level to deck level. That transition is most likely going to be either steps or a ramp. You can determine which it's going to be by considering which items you are going to be moving in and out.

Think about wheels and think about weight. If you have got a lot of wheeled items like wheelbarrows, lawnmowers, bicycles, and snowblowers, a ramp is going to make your life dramatically more pleasant. The same for heavy items: bags of concrete or potting soil, an air compressor, a table saw, and loads of firewood will all seem heavier and more unwieldy to carry up and down the stairs than they would to take up a ramp.

The downsides are that a ramp can take up a lot of real estate if your shed is high off of the ground. A set of well-designed stairs can also look much more classy than a utilitarian ramp. For every 6 inches of height the ramp needs to breach, it will need approximately 2 feet of length to keep the incline at a comfortable and safe pitch. If your deck is 18 inches high, you'll need a ramp about 6 feet long.

Before building anything, you'll need to identify the exact future location of your shed door and mark the opening clearly on the deck edge. For a typical-width single door of 30- to 36-inches, you'll want three vertical stringers supporting the ramp's deck boards. For a double-wide door, you need about five. You'll also need to locate the vicinity where the ramp will meet the ground. Excavate 2 inches down where each stringer will land and place a 2-inch patio block as a landing pad.

The stringers should be pressure-treated two-by-sixes or two-by-eights, as they will be in direct contact with the moisture-laden patio blocks. You'll also need a ledger 2x4 that you'll screw or bolt to the band joist. Cut the ledger to the width of your door opening and install it 2½ to 3 inches below the deck height, centered on the opening. Now cut your stringers to the appropriate length and notch them around the ledger.

Here's the tricky part: determining the ramp's exact length, and the appropriate angled cuts where the stringers will meet the shed and the patio blocks. Some quick geometry will provide the answers. Start with the vertical height of your deck off the ground and multiply by 4 to determine the horizontal length of the ramp. These two numbers are two sides of a right triangle. The ramp itself is the hypotenuse, which you can determine with the Pythagorean theorem of $A^2 + B^2 = C^2$.

If your deck height is 12 inches, then your horizontal ramp length is 48 inches, which makes your hypotenuse the square root of $(12 \times 12) + (48 \times 48)$, which equals 49.5 inches. In these proportions, the mitered angles at the top and bottom of the ramp will be approximately 15° and 75° respectively. Notch the upper (plumb) cut so the stringer will fit over and sit upon the ledger.

When you've got the stringers cut, screw them to the ledger and band joist using 2½- to 3-inch galvanized screws. About midway along your ledgers, install pressure-treated blocking between the stringers to solidify the frame and provide extra support for the decking. Then cut your decking to length. You can go the exact width of your ramp frame, or extend a few inches beyond if you'd like. You'll want to use pressure-treated two-by-sixes or two-by-eights to provide enough heft and sturdiness. Leave ¼- to ½-inch gaps between each decking board to allow precipitation and fallen leaves or pine needles to fall between the cracks. Screw them down to the stringers with 2½- or 3-inch galvanized screws.

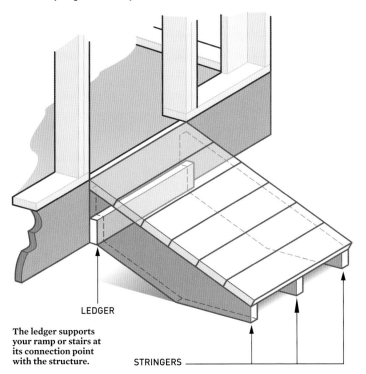

LEDGER

The ledger supports your ramp or stairs at its connection point with the structure.

STRINGERS

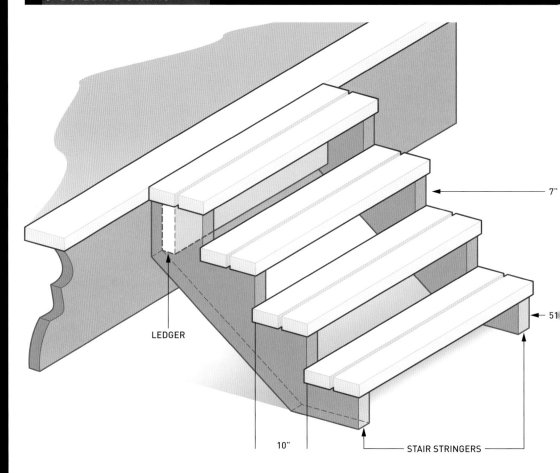

LEDGER

7"

51

10"

STAIR STRINGERS

**Take some time to determine
the appropriate dimensions
of the rise and run for your stairs.**

In all likelihood, unless you are building your shed on a precipice, you will need between one and three steps to get to deck height. You can take several routes to get the couple of steps you need. If you are looking to get some experience laying out and cutting a sawtooth, or notched, stringer, you'll need some pressure-treated two-by-twelves and a carpenter's square.

First, determine the distance from ground to deck to decide how many steps you will need. You should excavate two inches down and place patio blocks on which your stringers will sit for a sturdy foundation, but this shouldn't alter your ground height. Generally, a rise of between 6 and 7½ inches per step is in the range of normal. Anything outside of that spread makes for awkwardly shallow or dangerously steep steps.

If your deck height is between 15 and 18 inches, you're too tall for two steps and too short for three. In this situation, build up the ground at the base of the steps a couple of inches with soil, gravel, patio blocks, or a big flat stone.

If your deck height is 21 inches, you'll need three 7-inch risers or steps. A typical tread depth between risers is about 10 inches. With your carpenter square, measure off your risers and treads: 10 inches in, 7 inches up, 10 in, 7 up, 10 in, 7 up. To offset the thickness of the treads, cut off a strip equivalent to their thickness at the base of the stringer. If you use 2x material (which is only 1½ inches thick), you'll need to slice 1½ inches from the stringers where they meet the ground. Otherwise, your first step will be a toe-stubbing 8½ inches high.

Once you've got it all laid out, cut your first stringer, finishing each notch with a handsaw instead of your circular saw so you don't overcut. You can use this first stringer as a template to lay out any additional stringers. For a typical single door, you can get away with just two stringers, but for anything wider, you'll want additional strength. Also, you'll need to cut a ledger that

will fit between each stringer where the stairs meet the band joist. The ledger will tie your stairs to the shed deck.

When you've got the stringers in place and affixed to the deck, cut and add your treads. For a 10-inch tread depth, a pair of two-by-sixes will fit perfectly, with a small gap between them, and a small overhanging lip. The treads can be cut flush with the outer edge of the stringers, or overhang them by a couple of inches on either side. Screw them down with 2½- or 3-inch galvanized screws.

Another option we do not recommend is a cleated stringer, which attaches blocks

or cleats to the inside of two un-notched stringers, and then attaches the treads to the cleats. This set of stairs is less sturdy than the above and tends to fall apart after a few years of use.

A third option is to build a series of two-by-six boxes in diminishing dimensions and simply stack one on top of the next. Then add stair treads to cover the tops.

Whichever option you choose—ramp or stairs, cleated, notched, or boxes—don't skimp on materials. This part of your shed will face the most use, the most weather, and the most wear and tear.

A series of boxes, each approximately 10 inches smaller than the next, creates a simple stacked stair system.

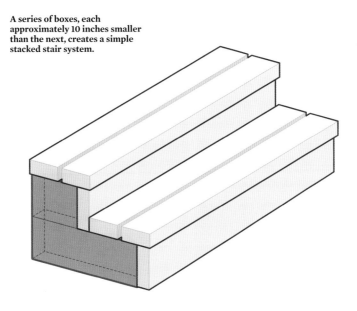

Framing
the Walls
and Roof

Wall and roof framing, even with window and door openings, can be cut, assembled, and raised in hours, or even faster for experienced carpenters.

CHAPTER 3

Design

Before embarking on the actual framing of your walls, draw up some construction documents detailing their structural make-up. To do this, pull out the exterior elevations you created earlier when you were at the design stage. This time, you'll draw the wall as if you've acquired X-ray vision, removing the sheathing and siding materials to show the undressed, framed skeleton beneath.

Your framing plan will enable you to determine how much material you need to order.

Start by redrawing the perimeter of each of your long walls, duplicating your measurements from the originals. Add another line just above the bottom to indicate your bottom plate. If each box on your graph paper equals 6 inches, the 1½-inch thickness of the plate will take up about a quarter of one box's height. Don't worry about it being exact. Along the top, you'll draw two top plates. Some sheds use only one top plate, but doubling it

will provide extra support for the roof structure above and provide an effective means of joining adjacent walls together. Next, add your wall joists, starting with the corner joist, then 15¼ inches to the next stud, and then 16 inches thereafter down the length of the wall. Draw in two additional studs on each end, inside your two end studs sanwiching three or four lengths of 2x4 blocking. This tripling up will provide a way to tie in your adjacent walls.

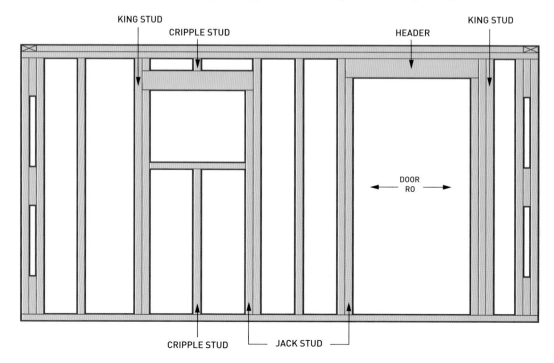

KING STUD

CRIPPLE STUD

HEADER

KING STUD

DOOR
RO

CRIPPLE STUD — JACK STUD

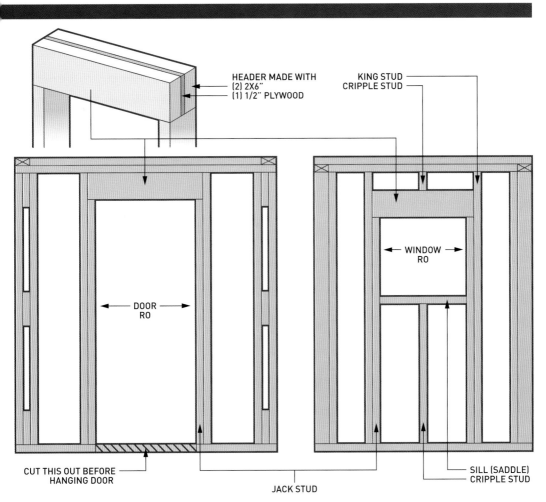

HEADER MADE WITH
(2) 2X6"
(1) 1/2" PLYWOOD

KING STUD
CRIPPLE STUD

WINDOW
RO

DOOR
RO

CUT THIS OUT BEFORE
HANGING DOOR

JACK STUD

SILL (SADDLE)
CRIPPLE STUD

Framing door and window openings requires careful thought and measurement.

Next, you'll draw in any window or door openings that will be part of that wall. If you haven't yet purchased or located your windows, you'll need to do this before you proceed, as you need to know the exact measurements. Assuming you've got them in hand, sketch in your rough opening (the space required to fit your entire window assembly, including the jambs) defined by a two-by-six (5½-inch-tall) header above, supported by two jack studs. If your jack studs aren't immediately adjacent to common wall studs, you'll need to add king studs to straddle your header assembly. If you're working with a window, draw in your saddle, which will toenail into the jack studs, and finally add upper and lower cripples, placed at the points where common studs would have been located if they had not been interrupted by the rough opening.

Go through the same process with your short walls, except that their length will be 7 inches shorter than the deck's width to allow them to fit snugly between the ends of the long walls. You don't need to triple up the end studs, either.

Framing the Walls

Now, with your framing plan in hand, it's time to begin cutting and assembling your first wall. Wall framing begins by cutting the lower top plate and the bottom plate (two-by-four lumber is perfectly adequate for shed-scale construction) for your first long wall. Their length should equal the length of your finished deck. Using the deck as a building platform, lay the top and bottom plates on their sides, adjacent to each other. To assure identical stud placement, measure and mark their layout simultaneously with an X delineating the location of your studs on each plate, spacing them 16 inches o.c., but with the first stud 15¼ inches from the end. Then lay out two more studs immediately inside each end stud.

If this wall will have any window or door openings, this is the time to determine their exact placement. Based on your framing plan, identify the location of the rough openings on your plates, and lay out any relevant jack, king, and cripple studs. Label them with a J, K, or C.

When you've got all these elements clearly laid out, fire up the circular saw and let the cutting begin. First, cut your full-length (common) studs and nail them in place through the top and bottom plates using 16d nails. At both ends of the wall, add to the initial studs two more studs—effectively making a triple stud in each corner. You can also use three or four foot-long scraps as spacers in place of the center stud of this sandwich. Whichever route you choose, nail it together using 8d nails, as well as through the plates.

Then cut and nail any full-length king studs to surround the door or window rough openings. Assemble your headers from two-by-sixes sandwiched around a ½-inch plywood spacer, making a 3½-inch-thick header (exactly the thickness of your two-by-four wall). Cut the two jack studs to the height of the top of the rough opening, nail these to the king studs so their bottom edges are flush, and secure these doubled studs to the floor plate at the rough-opening marks. Then, nail the header in place on the jack studs.

A triple stud, or two studs sandwiching foot-long spacers, will provide a place to tie your short and long walls together.

WALL FRAMING PRIMER

two-by-fours, two-by-sixes, two-by-eights, or two-by-tens depending on the span length. As a rule, all perimeter walls are load bearing, as are central walls running perpendicular to the floor joists. King studs are full-length studs that sandwich a header, and jack studs are shortened studs that support the header. The horizontal bottom of a window opening is a saddle or rough sill. Short studs above the header and below the sill are known as cripple studs.

Stud walls require bracing to stiffen them and prevent racking (moving out of square). Galvanized metal bracing bands are available, or the studs can be notched to accept a one-by-four running from bottom plate to top plate at approximately a 45° angle. Another option is to use ½-inch plywood or OSB panels as sheathing: their shear strength also acts as a brace.

While floor joists and roof rafters handle bending stresses, wall studs (as the vertically-placed and spaced lumber is commonly known) are under compression and carry the load above directly down to the foundation. Even in a two-story house, two-by-fours are adequate for this task, although sometimes you will see two-by-sixes and even two-by-eights used for studs. This is commonly done to create a deeper wall for more insulation rather than for strength.

Walls are generally built flat on the subfloor, then tipped up to vertical and nailed in place. The builder marks out the top and bottom (or sole) plates with stud spacing, allowing for windows, doors, and intersecting walls, if any. Every window, door, or other break in the framing sequence of a load-bearing wall (any wall that supports weight from above) requires a horizontal header —a beam that transfers the load above the opening to the studs. Headers are built with

For each window, you'll need to cut a saddle to the width of the rough opening. Lay out its location on the king studs and then toenail it in place. Unlike the header, which stands vertically, the saddle will sit flat. Make sure it's level. Then cut the cripples for above the door, and above and below the windows. Again, these should be located where your common studs would have fallen had it not been for the interruption by the rough opening. Nail through the top and bottom plates and toenail into the header. If toenailing from the sides proves difficult due to lack of space between the header and top plate, you can toenail from the front and back (after you stand the wall up).

Cut the second top plate 7 inches shorter than the first top plate and nail it centered on the first, 3-½ inches shy of each end. The upper top plate of your short walls will extend to this void, tying the two walls together here,

(bottom left) A header can utilize two by fours for a short span, but two by sixes will provide better structural support for the load above. (bottom right) A metal let-in brace prevents a wall from 'racking' in place of plywood sheathing.

but these will be added after the walls are standing.

If you will be sheathing with sheet goods, you are ready to move ahead. If you will be siding with board and batten, shiplap, or another non-structural material, you've got some work ahead of you still: adding some triangulation to prevent racking, as well as providing horizontal options to which vertically-oriented siding will be affixed.

WOOD LET IN BRACE SET IN NOTCHES

(above) A wood let-in brace requires notching studs and top and bottom plates. The amount of blocking allows for narrow vertical siding to be used.

To stiffen the wall, there are two options. The easiest is to utilize a metal let-in brace. These braces or straps come in both T and L profiles. With the wall still lying flat, check it for squareness, and then snap a chalk line at a 45° to 60° angle from top to bottom plate, avoiding rough openings. Then, with your circular saw, cut a kerf (a shallow slice) in each joist and plate on the line about 1/16 inch deeper than the leg of

the strap. Fasten the strap to the studs and plates following the manufacturers instructions.

The same basic concept applies with the use of a one-by-four or two-by-four wood let-in brace. In this instance, you'll need to snap two parallel chalk lines, matching the exact width of the brace. You'll then notch out the space between the lines by making a series of kerf cuts on each stud or plate at a depth of about 1/16 inch deeper than the thickness of the brace. Use a chisel to pop out the wood between each kerf. Then lay the one-by-four in the slots, affix it with two 8d nails into each stud and plate, and trim any excess length.

If you intend to sheath with horizontal channel shiplap or channel siding, you can jump to the next section. But if your

sheathing choice is vertical shiplap or board-and-batten siding, you'll also need to create some horizontal means by which you will fasten the siding to the wall, since both the siding and studs run vertically. There are three options. The easiest is to simply affix one-by-three spruce strapping horizontally the length of the wall at 8- to 12-inch intervals. The result will be siding that sits proud of the framing by the thickness of the strapping.

A more challenging route is to cut notches in the studs into which the strapping will sit, flush with the exterior of the framing, as with the diagonal bracing method described above. In this instance, these will run horizontally across the wall from 2- to 3-foot intervals.

(top) Notching the studs will allow horizontal nailers to sit flush, and accept nails from the coming vertical siding.

The most challenging option is to cut and place two-by-four or two-by-six blocking at intervals between the studs, flush with their outer edge. This requires a degree of care and patience as you cut them to length so they fit comfortably between each stud. Also, every other block can be nailed in place through the studs, but the intervening blocks will need to be toe-nailed because the adjacent block will prevent nailing access. Some people will get around this by staggering adjacent blocks up and down, but this creates the additional challenge of identifying exactly where your blocking is as you nail your siding to it.

Sheathing the wall before it is standing vertical—especially with sheet-good siding to which you will ultimately apply clapboards or shingles, or T-111 plywood, which serves as the siding—has a worthy advantage: gravity. It's much easier to affix plywood to your still-horizontal wall frame.

Make sure your wall is square, and then set the first piece of sheathing flush with the top plate and corner stud, running the sheet down four inches beyond the bottom plate so it will overlap with (and cover the seam between) the wall and deck framing below. Nail it with 8d nails approximately every 6 inches along the edges and every 10 inches elsewhere. Install the remaining sheets in the same fashion. You'll need to cut around any window and door openings.

(top) Install sheathing or sheet siding while the wall is still lying flat. (center) Use temporary braces to stand your walls vertically. (bottom) Screw the wall to the deck through the bottom plate.

You can also install your tongue-and-groove barn board or shiplap siding directly onto the framing without sheathing.

Each board can run long on the bottom by four inches or so. Make sure each board is tight with the previous board before nailing it.

Tip the wall up, making sure it is absolutely vertical, and have a helper secure it with temporary diagonal braces.

Screw the bottom plate to the decking with 3-inch deck screws, and nail through the siding into the band joist and sill. Then repeat the entire wall building, sheathing, and raising process with the opposite long wall.

For the short walls, which will be built 3½ inches shy on each end to allow for them to fit snugly between the long walls, run your sheathing (or your one-by-three

strapping in preparation for vertical siding) 3½ inches wide on each side to cover the ends of those long walls. You'll also run it 1½ inches tall to cover where you will ultimately add your upper top plate.

When you've got your short walls standing (removing the temporary braces as necessary),

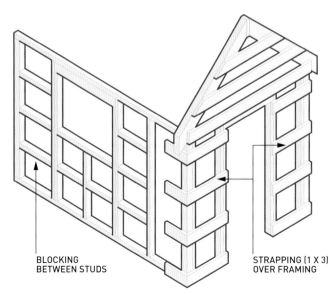

(top left) For additional holding power, screw the walls together at the corners rather than nailing them. (top right) The second top plate provides another opportunity to fasten walls together.

double-check for squareness and tie them in with the long walls by nailing through the corner studs into the blocking you created for this very purpose at the corners of the long walls.

Then cut your upper top plate for each of the short walls and nail it into place. Remember to cantilever it by 3½ inches on each end so it bridges the lower top plate of the long walls, where you'll also nail it down to further tie the walls together.

BLOCKING
BETWEEN STUDS

STRAPPING (1 X 3)
OVER FRAMING

SHED NATION CITIZEN

Working in construction, I get to build some great structures for other people. I decided to build this lighthouse/waterski shack as part of a project to improve my home. It reminds me of growing up in Michigan and boating on the Great Lakes. The lighthouse is on Lake Dunlap, near my home in south-central Texas. About 80 percent of the material is salvaged, some of it from an 1890 farmhouse. The front door is from a Navy ship, and took me four months to find. I used two-by-six wood studs and skip sheathing on the outside, and finished the exterior with Alaskan cypress tree shingles—they're maintenance-free and should age nicely.

The hardest part was designing each phase before I ever picked up a board. I drew and re-drew everything to scale until I got the design proportionally and aesthetically correct: 20 feet tall with an 11-foot base. When the design was complete, I built it as separate components and hoisted these into position. Inside, there are no ceiling joists, just a spiderweb of wooden beams, so you can see all the way up to the bottom of the roof. The wooden interior has built-ins for storage, a refrigerator, a marble countertop that extends through the wall to the outside, and a stereo/DVD system that is great when we have parties.

The whole project took about two years. The only problem is that when I come outside in the morning and see the lighthouse and the water, I feel so comfortable I don't want to leave. —*GARY VERLINDEN, TX*

Framing the Roof

There are two general options for roof framing: cutting and placing rafters into position one at a time, or building whole roof trusses on the ground and raising them as a unit. Building trusses for a house creates units of a scale and weight that require a crane to lift them in place. But for a typical shed, they can be lifted into place by a couple of people. And because much of the work occurs on the ground, this tends to be an easier, and safer, way to go.

Build trusses on a flat surface. This carpenter is building his trusses before wall construction which we do not advocate.

▶ ASSEMBLING ROOF TRUSSES

Building roof trusses is a simpler endeavor. The best approach is to use a jig laid out either on the shed floor or on a piece of plywood.

Draw a centerline across the plywood. Then, nail a straight 2 x 4 along the bottom of the plywood to serve as a stop for positioning the bottom chord of the truss. To make the bottom chord, cut a two-by-four to match the width of the shed. Don't forget to add the thickness of your sheathing and siding to that number. Mark its center as well.

To use a framing (or carpenter's) square to mark the angled cuts on the ends of the bottom chord, with the heel (right angle) of the square pointing away from you, align the 12-inch mark on the body blade (the thicker and longer arm) with a lower corner of the stock, and align the mark equal to your rise (8 inches, in this example) on the tongue (the shorter, thinner arm) along the bottom edge of the board. Scribe the angled edge

of the body blade, and repeat this process at the opposite end. Then cut to the lines.

With the bottom chord in place and centered, use your framing square to mark the top angled plumb cuts on two truss rafters. To do this, you do the opposite of what you just did with the bottom chord, aligning the 8-inch (or whatever your rise is) mark of the tongue in the bottom corner of your board, and the 12-inch mark along the bottom edge. Then draw a line along the tongue shaft. Repeat this with a second board, and make both cuts. Position the three pieces, and check that they're centered and meet properly. Then, nail two-by-four stops against the outside edges of the sloping members to aid in aligning the remaining trusses for assembly.

Cut the rafter tails at the desired angle, allowing for approximately a 4- to 8-inch overhang. The tails can be cut plumb or square, or given a more creative detail, but for simplicity

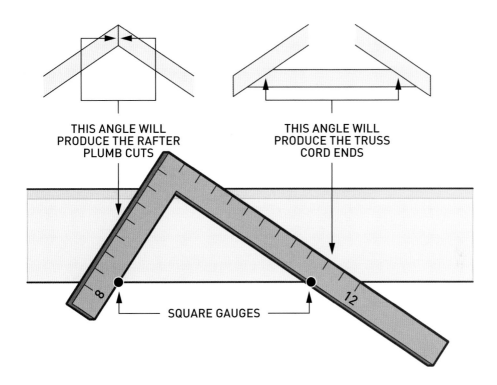

THIS ANGLE WILL
PRODUCE THE RAFTER
PLUMB CUTS

THIS ANGLE WILL
PRODUCE THE TRUSS
CORD ENDS

SQUARE GAUGES

Use the framing square to determine the angle cuts for your bottom cord and trusses.

of affixing fascia boards and trim later, a plumb cut will make your life easier. Assemble the trusses with ½-inch plywood gussets over each joint. A gusset is simply a plate (metal or plywood) that overlaps two butting structural members, tying them together. Your gussets should be large enough (approximately 8 × 12 inches before trimming angles) to provide room to put several nails into each member. Using construction adhesive before nailing with 1-inch roofing nails will help ensure the gussets'

effectiveness. Then you'll flip the whole assembly and add gussets to the other side, as well.

Note that the inner trusses are simple triangles with gussets on both sides. But for the two end trusses, you'll add vertical nailers on the outside for securing the siding, and gussets on the inside only. More on that in a moment.

For additional strength in a wider structure (12 feet or wider), you can add a king post, which is a vertical member running from the center of the bottom chord all the way up to the underside of the peak, making sure to scribe your cut

lines from the truss rafters themselves. You will also add an additional gusset at the base, along with two angled web members splaying from the center base up and out to the mid-point of the two rafters.

Once you've got all of your components for your first truss cut and fitting together, it makes sense to go into production mode, using the original framing members and gussets as templates, cutting all the rest at once.

For your two gable-end trusses, you'll affix two or three horizontal nailers with gussets at intervals between the bottom chord and the peak. And lastly,

A traditional gable is at the root of most roof designs. Though they are visually unique, a saltbox, shed, gambrel, and hip roof are variations on the gable theme, utilizing the gable's core elements. A gable roof is composed of rigid triangles, each made up of a ceiling joist and two rafters. A ridge beam ties the rafters at the peak and collar ties can be added to help prevent the load on the roof from spreading the rafters. Rafters can be spaced 16 or 24 inches apart, depending on the ceiling span and rafter pitch. The gable overhang is built with projecting lookouts that support fly rafters.

Roof pitch is expressed in inches. A roof that climbs 6 inches per lateral foot is said to be a 6 in 12 roof. Most roofs fall in the 4 in 12 to 12 in 12 range. Angled rafter cuts are laid out with a framing square. The notch cut to fit over the top plate of the wall is called a bird's mouth.

Trusses are made of lighter lumber than rafters and ceiling joists because truss design reduces bending stresses that call for wide stock. Trusses speed up the building process and allow longer unsupported spans. Truss components are assembled on the ground. They are tied together using plywood gussets or metal tie-plates and are raised into position as a unit.

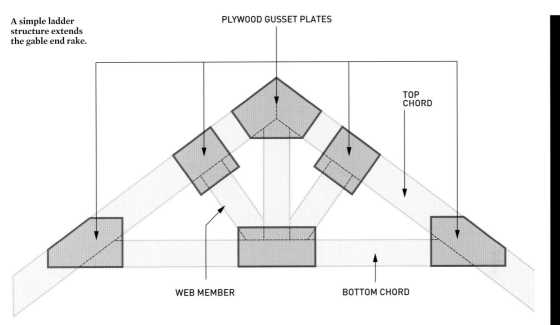

A simple ladder structure extends the gable end rake.

PLYWOOD GUSSET PLATES

TOP CHORD

WEB MEMBER

BOTTOM CHORD

you'll install a two-by-four shoe plate flush with the bottom of the chord, but butting out, away from the chord in an L. Screw through the chord to attach this. The shoe plate will enable you to affix the end rafters to the top plates of the walls below. Then add your sheathing while the trusses are still on the ground.

Finally, you'll need to add the rakes, the overhangs that extend out over each gable end. To do this, you will simply cut two more pairs of truss rafters for each end of the structure, along with approximately ten two-by-four blocks cut to the depth of your desired overhang. Place the blocks at 12-inch intervals between two matching rafters, forming a ladder, and screw the components together using 2½ inch decking screws. Then build

the adjacent unit and attach both sections to the exterior of the shed wall, perfectly aligned with the truss within, using 3-inch decking screws. Repeat the process for the other end wall.

A king post along with diagonal members adds dramatic strength to a truss.

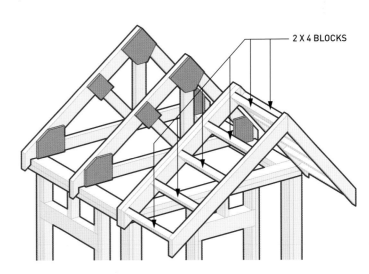

2 X 4 BLOCKS

Framing with rafters requires a degree of patience and skill, but it is wonderfully satisfying in its reliance on traditional methods. Rafters utilize a series of three special cuts: a plumb cut at the top, where the rafter will rest against the ridge board; a bird's mouth (actually a triangular wedge removed from the board by making two cuts, a heel cut and a seat cut), which allows the rafter to straddle the top plate of your wall; and the tail cut at the bottom of the eave.

The trick is to determine exactly where these cuts should be made. The plumb and tail cuts are fairly straightforward,

but the bird's mouth requires some attention to detail and a basic understanding of how to use a framing square.

The process begins with the laying of ceiling joists spanning from top plate to top plate, spaced at 24 inches o.c. Using a ladder, first lay out the locations of your joists and rafters in pairs on your top plates. Flush with the outer edge of the short-wall framing on one end of the structure, mark the location of your first rafter, with your first ceiling joist immediately adjacent. Lay out your next rafter/joist pairing 23¼ inches from the end of the structure,

and then continue down the top plate at 24-inch intervals from there. For the final pairing, flip the order, so your joist is first and your rafter is flush with the end of the framing below. If your interval is not exact when you get to the far end, remember that it is better to have an extra short interval than one that is too long.

Cut all of your joists to length. For a typical shed structure, two-by-four stock is perfectly adequate for the joists, though for a larger structure with a greater span, you would use two-by-sixes or even two-by-eights. And if you intend to store particularly heavy items up on the joists, you might consider two-by-sixes to handle the extra load. Before you begin installing the joists, measure the structure for squareness from top plate corner diagonally to the other top plate corner, and compare with the opposite pair. Assuming you've got a square and level

PLUMB CUT

RIDGE BEAM

RAFTER

SEAT CUT

BIRD'S MOUTH CUT

DOUBLE TOP PLATE

HEEL CUT

TAIL CUT

WALL STUD

Each rafter requires plumb and tail cuts at the top and bottom, and a bird's mouth (consisting of a seat and heel cut) at the top plate.

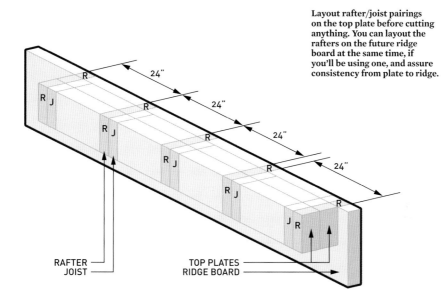

Layout rafter/joist pairings on the top plate before cutting anything. You can layout the rafters on the future ridge board at the same time, if you'll be using one, and assure consistency from plate to ridge.

24"

24"

24"

24"

RAFTER
JOIST

TOP PLATES
RIDGE BOARD

deck, and square and plumb walls, you should be fine. But if the measurements are off, you'll need to push and pull the structure into square.

Lay your joists on their marks on the top plates and toenail them in place using 8d nails. The joists play an integral role in the roof structure, counteracting the outward, lateral force prompted by the weight of the rafters, ridge beam, roof sheathing, roofing material, and the potential snow-load above, all of which seek to flatten the roof like a pancake by pushing the walls out.

Next, you'll begin preparing your rafters. This is where

things get a little complicated. To determine your base rafter length, it's geometry time again. Remember the Pythagorean theorem for right triangles? $A^2 + B^2 = C^2$. Since the vertical rise and horizontal run of your pitch are known, and they form a right angle, then the hypotenuse closing in the triangle will equal your rafter length. For example, let's assume your roof pitch is 8 in 12, and you've got a 10-foot-wide shed span. That means your run—half your span—is 5 feet, or 60 inches. With an 8-inch rise per foot, that means you've got an overall rise of 40 inches over the course of the run. Insert those totals into

the Pythagorean Theorem and you've got 40×40 (1600) plus 60×60 (3600) which equals 5200. Then take the square root of that, for a rafter length of 72.1 inches.

Keep in mind this length is equal only to the distance from the ridge to the outer edge of the top plate of the wall. Assuming your shed calls for an eave, you'll need to extend the rafter and overhang the wall. It is up to you how much of an overhang you want, but keep in mind that the further it overhangs, the lower it gets, which could become an obstacle for doors or foreheads below. Generally a 4- to 8-inch overhang would be in keeping with the scale

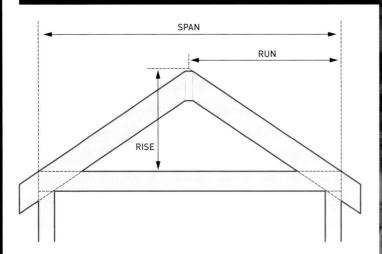

Rise squared times run squared equals the square of your rafter length from ridge to the outer edge of the wall framing atop the top plate.

of a structure this size. With this ridge-to-eave measurement, you now know the length of the boards you will use as a starting point for your rafters.

To lay out the location and angles of the three cuts each rafter (see page 96), make the will need, you'll use your framing square. Also helpful are two "square gauges" (sometimes referred to as "stair gauges"), which clamp onto the framing square allowing for repeated marking of the same angle.

After stepping off your rafter, (see page 96) make the appropriate cuts. On the bird's mouth, only use the circular saw to the point where the heel and seat cut lines intersect. Then finish the job with a handsaw. Assuming you've done the job right, you are done with the framing square. You can simply use your first rafter as a template for the remaining rafters. But first, create one duplicate rafter so you have a pair, and check your work. Attach a temporary 2x block (mimicking the thickness of your as-yet un-created ridge board) to the end of one of the rafters, and with a helper, put the two rafters in position. Assuming they sit appropriately snugly on the top plates and against the ridge board scrap, you are in business. Pull them back down and cut the rest of your rafters. Cut two extra pairs for the rakes (overhangs on the gable ends), but these—sometimes called fly rafters—won't need a bird's mouth, as they will not rest on the top plate.

STEPPING OFF RAFTER CUTS

Lay a straight two-by-six board flat on the ground with the crown side away from you. Place the framing square near the right-hand end of the board, with the point (or heel) facing you, the tongue (thinner, shorter arm) heading away angled to the right, and the body (thicker, longer arm) angled off to the left. Align the figure for your unit run— 12 inches, in the current example—found on the outside edge of the square's body, and the figure for your unit rise—8 inches, in the current example—found on the outer edge of the framing square's tongue, so that both meet along the rafter's far edge. Then attach and tighten the square gauges along the inner edges of the framing square so they will keep the square at that exact angle any time the gauges rest against the edge of the board.

Draw a line along the outer edge of the tongue. Also draw a line along the outer edge of the body. Then slide the framing square down along the rafter until the tongue's 8-inch mark meets the end of the body line you just drew. Make sure your gauges are still resting against the rafter edge, and draw another line along the outer edge of the body. Continue down the rafter—marking the increments in an identical way—the number of steps equivalent to your run (in the case of our example, five steps for our 5-foot run), and

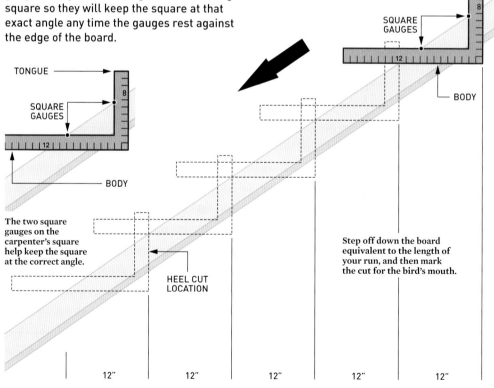

TONGUE

SQUARE GAUGES

8

12

BODY

TONGUE

SQUARE GAUGES

8

12

BODY

The two square gauges on the carpenter's square help keep the square at the correct angle.

HEEL CUT LOCATION

Step off down the board equivalent to the length of your run, and then mark the cut for the bird's mouth.

12"   12"   12"   12"   12"

then mark a line down the tongue which will indicate the "heel" cut for your bird's mouth.

To mark the seat cut for the bird's mouth, with the framing square still in position at your fifth step, note the exact measurement along the outside edge of your square's body, from the point where the body and tongue meet to the location where the body meets the rafter's bottom edge (let's say 4 inches in this example). Add this number to the width of your top plate (if you used a two-by-four, it's 3½ inches), for a total of 7½ inches. Now slide your framing square in the opposite direction you've been stepping off, until the 7½ inch mark on the outside of the square's body aligns with your heel cut line. Draw a line from the heel cut line to the right along the body to the board's edge. This is your seat cut line, at a perfect 3½ inches to sit neatly on your top plate.

If your run is an uneven increment—let's say 5'6"—at your fifth step, extend the line along the body an extra 6 inches, make a mark, slide your square down the rafter until the tongue meets this mark, and draw a heel cut down to the board's edge. Then follow the directions above to find your seat line.

For your tail cut, slide down the desired distance beyond the bird's-mouth notch you just drew, and mark your cut line. Here you have some leeway. Your rafter tail can be cut horizontally along the body line, vertically along the tongue line, or a combination of these, or you can even make an artistic statement with curves, a zig-zag, or whatever floats your boat—though keep in mind that the more complicated your tail, the more time consuming it will be, multiplied by the number of rafters you need to cut, and the more challenging it might be to affix fascia trim.

You're almost ready to make some cuts. But you need to do one more thing. Back up at the other end, you drew your very first tongue line, which in theory should be your plumb cut. But that assumes that the rafter is at full length. In fact, it is not. The rafter will butt into a ridge beam, and that ridge board has a thickness (1½ inches) that must be taken into account. But since half of the ridge board will be on this half of the structure and half will be on the other, each rafter will only need to be shortened by ¾ inch. So draw a line parallel to the first one, ¾ inch to the inside.

Slide the square to the right until the appropriate body measurement meets your heel cut line.

7 6 5 4 3 2 1

10 9 8 7 6 5 4 3 2 1

SEAT CUT

HEEL CUT

MEASURE HERE
PLUS 3 1/2

Various rafter tail options.

AXON

PROFILE

Raising rafters or trusses is another exciting moment in the shed-building process, where dramatic progress occurs relatively quickly. If you've pre-built trusses, it will be especially quick. With some helpers, carry one of the gable end trusses upside down through the door and into your shed, and then lift it so that each rafter tail is resting up on the top plate near the end wall, rake end facing toward you. The unit should hang there, upside down. Then with your two helpers on ladders in the corners, carefully flip the peak up and into place.

Two people should be able to easily move the gable end trusses into the shed. (right) Rest the unit upside down with the exterior side facing in.

With your helpers holding it steady, check its placement, and then screw down through the shoe plate on the truss into the top plate below with 3-inch decking screws every 8 to 10 inches. Repeat the process with the opposite end gable.

Next, lay out the location of the inner trusses at 24 inches o.c. on the top plates, and begin lifting them into place one at a time.

These trusses should be light enough to hoist up on one side of the structure and slide across the top of your framing. Screw them down into the top plate at an angle with 3-inch screws. Finally, take a one-by-four and cut it to the length of your structure. Temporarily screw

it in place running from truss rafter to truss rafter, just above the top plate, and mark the center point of each rafter on it. Then unscrew it and slide it up to just below the peak of the structure, and screw it into your end trusses. Then move from truss to truss, aligning them with the marks you made, and screwing one-by-four down with 2-inch screws. This will keep the trusses temporarily in position until you add sheathing.

If you've opted to cut individual rafters rather than trusses, the challenge is getting the end rafters and ridge board in position and stable. Once you've done that, raising the rest of the rafters is quick and painless.

The first task is to create a safe platform on which to work by screwing down a temporary row of plywood sheets along the middle of your ceiling joists. Next, cut your two-by-six ridge board to length—equivalent to the length of your building, plus the distance you wish your rakes (gable-end eaves) to extend out beyond each end. If the length you need is longer than your longest board, you can butt two boards end to end, but make sure that joint corresponds with a rafter location. Lift your ridge board up onto your ceiling joists

Seat the gable end rafter with the shoe plate directly on the top plate. (right) The inner trusses can be handed up from the side of the structure.

and lay it flat on the joists so that you can lay out all of your rafter locations on one side. Then flip it and lay out the rafter locations for the other side.

Next, attach two temporary two-by-four braces on each end of the structure: one rising vertically from the outside edge of the top plate and joists beneath just off center, the other supporting the first at a diagonal. Make sure the first is tall enough to provide support for the coming rafters. With a helper, raise your first end rafter, one of you making sure the rafter is flush with the end of the structure and that the bird's mouth is sitting snug on the end of the top plate. The other of you

will hold the plumb cut end up in position and measure up from the top plate to make certain that you are at the correct height (refer back to your Pythagorean rafter calculations). Note that the true peak is an imaginary point just a little bit above the flat edge atop the ridge board. Toenail the rafter to the top plate with two 8d nails, and then tack the rafter to the two-by-four brace. Repeat this process on the gable at the opposite end. If you are using two ridge boards, just move your operation in to the joist that is one back from where your ridge boards will butt, and add a temporary vertical brace up just off the center of that joist. Then, raise

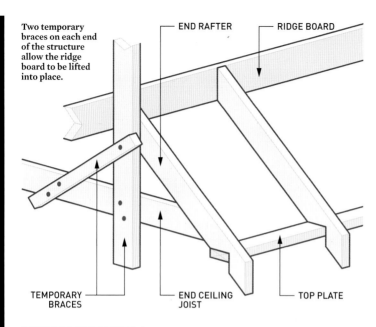

Two temporary braces on each end of the structure allow the ridge board to be lifted into place.

END RAFTER

RIDGE BOARD

TEMPORARY BRACES

END CEILING JOIST

TOP PLATE

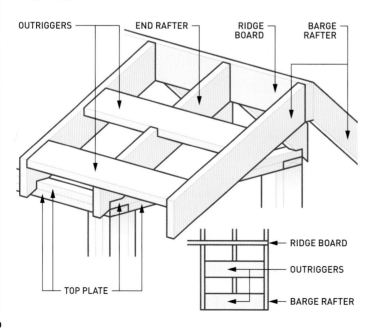

Outriggers cantilevered beyond the end rafter support the rake end {or barge} rafters.

OUTRIGGERS

END RAFTER

RIDGE BOARD

BARGE RAFTER

TOP PLATE

RIDGE BOARD

OUTRIGGERS

BARGE RAFTER

the ridge board into place on both ends and nail it through the backside of the ridge board with three 16d nails, first on one end and then on the other.

Check to make sure your ridge is level. Now you'll affix the sister rafters, toenailing them into place on the ridge board with three 3½-inch nails. If you need to add a second length of ridge board, start at the opposite end, and cover the junction where the ridge boards meet with rafters. The remainder is pretty straightforward, adding pairs from one end to the other. Then go back and drive three 3-inch nails through each rafter and into the floor joist where they intersect just above the top plate.

To add the rake, you'll need to create outriggers that span from the second rafter through a notch in the end rafter and extend out over the end of the structure 1½ inches less than your ridge board cantilever do. Spacing the outriggers about every 3 feet, and using care to make certain that they're flush with the top sides of the rafters, butt them against the second rafter (nailed through the back side of the rafter with 3½-inch nails), and then pass them through a notch in the end rafter that you'll create by making a series of shallow kerf cuts and chiseling out the remnants. You'll nail straight down into the end rafter with more 3½-inch nails. Then, with a helper, cap the ends of the outriggers with your rake rafters (the ones without the bird's mouths), and toenail them flush with the end of the ridge board.

You need something to nail your sheathing to in the gable end, so remove the temporary vertical braces that held up the end rafters, and add two horizontal two-by-four nailers—spanning the end rafter pairs—evenly spaced between the top plate and the peak. Then continue your sheathing material up to the rafters, fastened to the horizontal nailers.

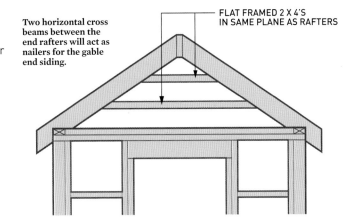

Two horizontal cross beams between the end rafters will act as nailers for the gable end siding.

FLAT FRAMED 2 X 4'S IN SAME PLANE AS RAFTERS

SHED NATION CITIZEN

This Tudor cottage was modeled after a centuries-old version in the British countryside.

While vacationing in the Cotswolds region of Great Britain several years ago, I came across the quintessential English Tudor cottage. The centuries-old building had dark, exposed timbers contrasted by bright white stucco panels. The first-floor walls were built of rough-cut rock and mortar. I snapped a picture of it before returning home to Minnesota.

A few years later, a large oak tree fell in the backyard. I decided then and there that I'd harvest that old tree and build a potting shed based on the cottage I'd seen in England. Using the photograph as a guide and a portable sawmill to slice up the oak, I devoted a year to constructing this 8 × 10 foot building.

I fabricated all of the shed's windows, including a pair of arched casements on the first floor and a second-story box bay that's located directly over the front door. The box bay lets in a lot of natural light and creates a comfortable window seat for my grandkids. I added a traditional Dutch door entryway and painted shutters, and incorporated a pull-down attic staircase for access to the second floor. The walls of the first floor are built of sandstone-like blocks that resemble natural stone but are made of concrete. The second story has a faux-stucco finish made of white painted plywood outlined in dark brown trim.

On the right side of the shed, I built a modest 5 × 8 foot greenhouse, which my wife and I use for starting plants in preparation for Minnesota's short growing season. The interior of the shed is outfitted with a wood-burning fireplace and a circa-1920 three-burner gas stove.

—TOM SCHROEDER, MN.

▶ SHEATHING AND ROOFING

Before sheathing the roof, you will need to do some finish work on the eaves and rake. First, you'll affix an eave fascia board by running a 1x along the ends of the rafter tails on each side of the shed. The height of the 1x depends on the width of the rafter tails it will cap. You will want to, at a minimum, cover the exposed end grain, and likely add an extra inch or so below to draw water down away from the rafter end.

If your rafter ends are cut vertical to the ground, lay a straight edge down along the top of each rafter, overhanging the rafter end by a few inches. Then slide the eave fascia board up the rafter tail until its top outside corner is flush with the plane of the top edge of the rafter, and nail it off with 8d nails. Do this with each rafter down the line. Cut the eave fascia board on the ends flush with the outer edge of the gable-end rafters. Now repeat on the opposite eave.

Next, cap your rakes with 1x rake fascia, running it flush with

the top edge of the rafter, and out beyond the rafter tails by ¾ inch to cover the exposed end of the eave fascia you just affixed to the rafter tails. You'll need to determine the height of the

(left) Skip sheathing allows for air circulation beneath the roof shingles. (right) The fascia board caps the ends of the rafters.

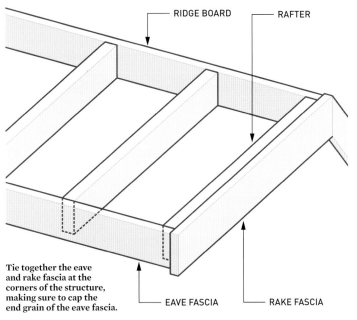

RIDGE BOARD   RAFTER

Tie together the eave and rake fascia at the corners of the structure, making sure to cap the end grain of the eave fascia.

EAVE FASCIA   RAKE FASCIA

rake board by ensuring that the angled tail cut completely caps the eave fascia. You'll also need to determine the exact angles of the tail and plumb cuts, based on the equivalent angles of those cuts on the gable-end rafter beneath.

Then move to the opposite gable end and repeat. You'll come back and add a round of eave and rake trim after sheathing the roof.

How you sheathe the roof depends on the roofing material you intend to use. For asphalt

shingles, tile, or slate, you will use ½-inch exterior grade plywood. For cedar shingles or shakes, you will need to skip sheathe the roof with 1x boards. Either sheathing method is appropriate for metal roofing.

→ **SKIP SHEATHING.** This entails running 1x boards horizontally across the rafters, leaving spaces between to allow for air to circulate beneath the shingles or shakes, promoting drying.

To skip sheathe, you need to place each board in a specific location to guarantee there will be something into which the shingles can be nailed. This depends on the amount of shingle you intend to expose to the elements. A fairly typical spacing plan allows for 5 inches of exposure for a 16- or 18-inch shingle. Use one-by-three (2½-inch-wide) spruce strapping as your sheathing material. To create the appropriate nailing platform for your shingles, you'll nail a one-by-three board flush with (and in no way extending beyond) the vertical plane of your eave fascia board. Cut it to length flush with the outside edges of the rake fascia boards. Nail it off with 2½-inch nails. Now add two more one-by-threes and one ripped 2-inch board, each butting tight with the preceding one. Next, using a one-by-three as a spacer, alternate one-by-threes and 2½-inch gaps all the way up the roof.

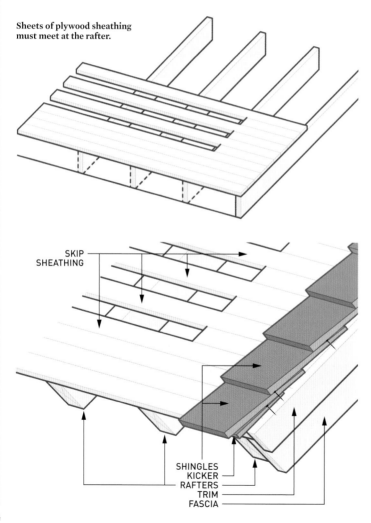

**Sheets of plywood sheathing
must meet at the rafter.**

SKIP
SHEATHING

SHINGLES
KICKER
RAFTERS
TRIM
FASCIA

Up at the ridge, you can return to solid sheathing for the final three courses. Finally, measure the distance from your last structural rafter to your gable ends, and cut enough appropriate one-by-three lengths to fill the gaps, in effect solid sheathing the gable end rake overhangs from top to bottom.

Now you'll return to your fascia work, wrapping first the eave fascia and then the rake fascia

with 1x trim. You'll want to rip two eave boards in the 2- to 4-inch range, and then place each one above the top edge of the eave fascia beneath, but not so high that it breaks the plane extending down along the top side of the sheathing. Lay a straight edge down from the sheathing to be certain. The trim board ends should be flush with the outside edges of the rake fascia. Then add 1x rake trim flush to the top of the sheathing,

Lay the remaining courses with a 5 inch reveal.

and out far enough and tall enough for the tail cut to cover the end grain of the eave trim you just applied.

→ **CEDAR SHINGLES.** These shingles will need two stacked courses along the bottom of the eave to assure against water penetration, and then new rows every five inches. Remember

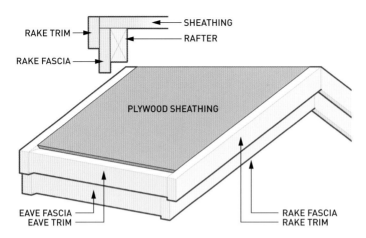

RAKE TRIM →
RAKE FASCIA →
SHEATHING ←
RAFTER ←
PLYWOOD SHEATHING
EAVE FASCIA
EAVE TRIM
RAKE FASCIA
RAKE TRIM

Install the eave and rake trim prior to installing the roofing material.

that the thick end of the shingle always points down-roof, and the tapered edge always up-roof. If you are using shakes with one rough and one smooth side, lay the rough side facing up. The first course should overhang the edge of the outer fascia board by 1½ inches—providing a drip edge—and by ½ to 1 inch on the rake ends. With two 1½-inch shingle nails, you'll nail the starter course 5 inches from their butt, or bottom, edges, with each nail about an inch in from the shingle's side edges. Leave a ¼-inch space between shingles to allow for expansion. The second course will sit almost directly on top of the starter course. You can actually drop the butt end ¼- inch below the starter course, which will help facilitate the drip edge function.

Make sure to stagger the vertical breaks between courses by at least 2 inches to prevent

water seepage. Nail the second course 6 inches from its butt end, thereby avoiding potential nail-on-nail collisions with the previous course.

The third course will begin 5 inches up from the butt end of course number 2, again nailing 6 inches from the bottom, ensuring that the nails will be hidden by the next course.

Snapping chalk lines will help you keep your courses lined up and eliminate a lot of tedious measuring. Continue in this fashion up to the peak, cutting off the top edge of the upper couple of courses at the ridge line, as needed.

When you've got the second half of the roof finished, build a simple ridgecap by nailing and gluing two cedar boards together in an L shape. Use a one-by-four and a one-by-six ripped to the appropriate width so that the two legs of the L are

equal. Fasten the cap atop the ridge by driving 2½-inch nails into each truss or rafter.

→ **PLYWOOD SHEATHING.** As with skip sheathing, this requires the installation of some fascia boards first. Starting with the eave sides, cap the rafter ends with a fascia board running flush between the outside edges of the gable end rafters, and sitting up to, but not breaking beyond, the plane of the rafter tops. Then install the rake fascias flush with the rafter tops and covering the ends of the eave fascias. Now you can lay your sheathing in courses horizontally, the first one laying flush with, and not beyond the plane of, the outer edges of both the eave and rake fascia. Nail

Sheets of plywood sheathing must meet at the rafter.

the first board off on the gable end rafter first and then double check that it's square with the eave fascia before nailing the rest. Make sure your board ends meet midway on a rafter so they can both be nailed off.

Remember to stagger your sheets so they don't meet at any four-corner intersections. Use 8d galvanized nails spaced 6 in. apart. When you get to the ridge, rip the sheathing so it's an inch or so short of the peak on each side. This will get covered with a ridge cap and allow for venting. When you've sheathed both sides of the roof, circle back and add first your eave and then rake trim boards, being careful to not break the plane of the top of the sheathing.

You have the option of rolling out and stapling down roofing felt, at this point. Some builders skip this step, but it is a fairly inexpensive and quick endeavor that will pay off in the long run by helping to keep water out of the structure. Roll layers out starting at the eave, and overlap each successive layer atop the previous run by 4 to 6 inches or so.

→ **ASPHALT SHINGLES.**
Whether architectural or 3-tab, these shingles require the roof edge to be trimmed with drip edges. A drip edge is a T-shaped galvanized metal sheet. You'll slide one end of the T up under the roofing felt at the eaves, until the bottom of the T is snug up against the fascia trim, and then nail it down to the sheathing. Next, add the rake drip caps on top of the felt. You can trim the ends to length with a tin snip.

Begin roofing by rolling out an asphalt starter strip along the eave so it overhangs about ½ inch. Install the shingles from one edge, using the spacing recommended by the manufacturer. At the edges, let the shingles overhang the drip edge by ¼ inch.

Trim away shingles that cover the 2-inch ventilation space at the peak. Then center the ridge vent and tack it in place with roofing nails. Ridge vents are produced by numerous companies. Check at your local lumberyard or home building center. You'll cover the vent with cap shingles, starting on one end of the ridge with 1¾-inch roofing nails. Install the second over the first leaving the recommended exposure, and continue across the roof's ridge.

→ **METAL ROOFING.** This can be installed atop either plywood sheathing (along with roofing felt) or skip sheathing (without the felt). If you opt for a standing seam roof, you'll want to bring in professionals to install the drip edges and the roofing itself. But for metal panels, the DIYer can still forge ahead. The sheets come in various widths but most often are 3 feet wide. Many

(top) Drip edge and a starter strip underlay the first courses of shingle. (bottom) Cap shingles cover the ridge vent.

lumber yards can order them pre-cut to a specific length, which will simplify your life tremendously. If not, you can cut the metal using a circular saw with a metal-cutting abrasive blade. For steel sheets, screw into the flat part of the roof panels using hex-head roofing screws with neoprene washers. For aluminum sheets, use aluminum roofing nails through the high rib of the panel. Don't mix steel and aluminum as the combo will cause galvanic action, leading to corrosion in the aluminum.

Details
and
Finishing

It's time to move ahead to the next stage. Apply the finishing touches and attend to the details that will make your shed watertight, fully functional, and attractive.

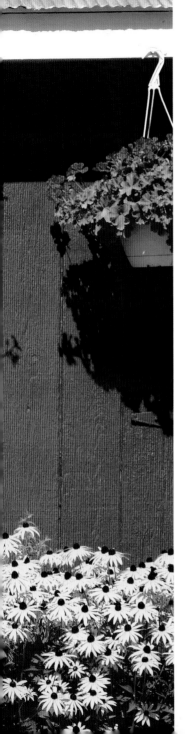

Siding, Trim and Window Installation

Window, trim, and siding installation are inextricably linked. In some instances, it's necessary to install the siding first, and then the windows and window trim. In others, you will install your windows and window trim first, and then butt your siding up against that. The variations depend on the type of windows and the type of siding you choose. (If you plan to use metal or vinyl siding, follow the manufacturer's installation directions.) To help you better understand which scenario will work with your shed, consider your window and siding choices.

For cost purposes, buying simple, single-pane sash windows at the local architectural salvage store, materials re-use center, or even lumber yard can be remarkably inexpensive. These can be mounted either with permanent stops to hold them in a fixed position, or with a hinge to allow for ventilation.

WINDOW PRICES

Windows are not cheap. As of mid-2009, new double-pane windows ranged from $150 to $1000, depending on size, material, and style. Single-pane windows cost less: in the $100 to $500 range. In general, vinyl-clad windows are the least expensive, followed by aluminum and then wood. Fixed pane windows are cheaper than any windows with a ventilation mechanism.

A budget-minded shed builder should consider used windows from an architectural salvage or materials re-use center. These can be in great shape for a fraction of the cost of new windows.

CASEMENT

AWNING

HINGED-IN

→ **CASEMENT WINDOWS.**
Casement windows sit on vertical hinges allowing them to swing or crank out as a door would open.

Pros:
- Since the entire window opens, they allow for full ventilation.
- The swing variety requires simple hardware: hinges and a latch.
- Opening to the outside means no likelihood of interfering with interior activities.

Cons:
- Because the free swing variety is opened by hand, a screen is challenging as it blocks access.
- The mechanism on the crank variety can deteriorate, and the removable crank handles can be misplaced or get stripped over time.

→ **AWNING WINDOWS.**
Awning windows are like casements but hinged on top so they swing up and out at the bottom.

Pros:
- Same as casements.
- An open awning window can act as a canopy, keeping rain out while open.

Cons:
- Same as casements
- The free swing variety requires a latch or support mechanism to keep window in open position.

→ **HINGED WINDOWS.**
The opposite concept of the awning window, these are hinged along the inside bottom so they tilt in at the top. These can be allowed to swing down all the way to horizontal, or designed with a stop to allow for minimal ventilation. They are kept closed with a simple latch along the top.

Pros:
- The simple hinge and latch mechanisms are easy to install and maintain.
- They can be used with exterior screens or storm windows.
- Full ventilation is provided if no stops are installed.
- They can be created from a simple sash window.

Cons:
- They are less weather tight than others, especially if home-made.

DOUBLE HUNG

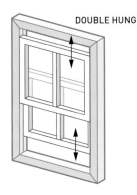

SLIDER

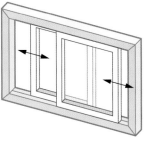

FIXED

→ **SINGLE- AND DOUBLE-HUNG.**
Double-hung windows have two overlapping panes, one above and one below, that move up or down to overlap each other. A single-hung window is the same concept, but only the lower sash is operable.

Pros:
- The vertical design eliminates the need for hinges, latches and crank mechanisms.
- They can be used with screens or storm windows.
- Traditional look.

Cons:
- You can never open more than half the window's surface area at a time.
- Humidity and weather changes can cause sticking.

→ **SLIDER WINDOWS.**
Sliders are a variant of a single-hung, but with the pane sliding horizontally in a track rather than vertically.

Pros:
- They can be used with screens or storm windows.

Cons:
- Rollers along bottom track can get gummed up preventing a smooth slide.
- You can never open more than half the window's surface area at a time.

→ **FIXED WINDOWS.**
Fixed windows are set in place with no ventilation.

Pros:
- They are the most effective at preventing moisture and air seepage.
- No mechanism or moving parts means less potential need for repair.
- They are the cheapest option.

Cons:
- There is no opportunity for ventilation.

Windows can also be discussed in the context of what is included in the overall window unit. Windows can be bought with a flange that extends over the sheathing on the exterior of the house and allows for simple attachment. Or they can be ordered with jambs and casing—wood, aluminum, fiberglass, or vinyl trim and sill already attached. Or if you prefer to build your own jambs and casings, you can simply purchase the window sash, the glass itself with a basic frame.

Each of these options offers pros and cons. If you were building a house, considerable time would be spent mulling these over. But in the case of a simple shed, the options should be simplified to the consideration of function (should they open, and if so, how?) and cost (what's the budget?). If your shed will be used predominantly for storage, simple fixed windows are probably your best bet. But if you will be using the structure for an activity, and hence be spending more substantial time in it, a simple mechanism that allows for ventilation should be considered.

Another consideration is whether you intend to insulate the structure. If you have thoughts of insulating the space with heat or adding air conditioning— perhaps as a workshop or art studio—you will want to purchase double-pane windows that will provide insulative value. But for most simple storage sheds, single-pane windows are more than adequate.

If you already used T-111 plywood or another sheet good siding in place of sheathing, you can install a window with a flange or casing directly on top of the siding. If you will be siding with solid wood, vinyl or metal siding, put the windows in first.

→ **LEVELING THE UNIT.** Window installation is fairly straight-forward. The biggest concern is making sure the unit is level. If you are working with windows clad with a flange or casings, simply slide the unit into your rough opening from the outside, and then with a 9-inch or 2-foot level, move inside and shim around the window between the jambs and the rough opening to make certain the window is level and square and that it fits snugly in place. If you need to you can drive a nail into one of the top corners of the casing or flange to keep it from dropping out while you fiddle with it.

→ **FASTENING THE WINDOW.** When you've got the window shimmed and level, move back outside and nail through the flange or exterior trim and into the header, sill plate, and jack studs with galvanized roofing nails if fastening through a flange, or with 8d finish nails through casings. Then head back inside and nail through the jambs

Use shims between the jambs and rough opening framing to maneuver the window into square.

and shims into the adjacent studs with 8d finish nails.

→ **SASH WINDOW.** For a simple sash window, construct and install the jambs that will surround the sash using 1X cedar. The jambs should extend out flush with the exterior of the sheathing, and in as deep as flush with the inside of the surrounding framing members, but could be less. To do this, and assuming your windows are ready to install, take an accurate measurement of them and compare it with your rough opening. You should have just enough room for a ¾-inch gap

all the way around for your jambs. If you have more than another ¼-inch of wiggle room you'll probably need to do some shimming to close the gap by nailing up some thin spacers.

→ **FIRST CUT YOUR SILL TO LENGTH.** Unlike the sides and top, which will have simple 90° cuts at each end, you have the option of creating a longer sill, with the flourish of wrapping out beyond the perimeters of the window width, usually to the outside edges of what will be your casing (or a little beyond), once you've installed it. This is a nice aesthetic touch created

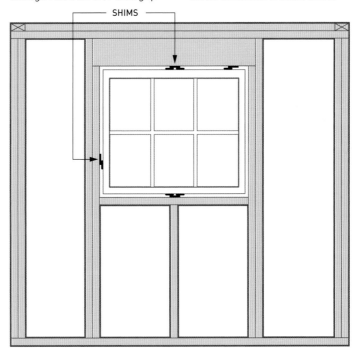

SHIMS

A small dowel plug will act as a perfect stop for the window. (bottom left) Notch the sill with a circular or table saw, but finish the job with a handsaw so you don't overcut.

by simply notching around the outside of the sheathing for a couple extra inches, and perhaps rounding or shaping the outside corner of the sill before it returns to the wall.

The complicating factor is that the sill will be prone to rot because water will collect there, so it is necessary to bevel or angle the sill between 5° and 15° with your table saw to prompt drainage.

Once you've got your sill squared away, measure and nail up your top jamb and then cut your side jambs to fit. Use 8d finish nails all around. If it's going to be a fixed window, you'll want to add narrow wood stops on the interior of the frame to hold the sash in place.

The exterior trim can act as the stop on the outside of the sash if it overlaps the sash by ½ inch. If you intend to allow the window to hinge completely, you won't need the stops. Instead you'll install hinges on the top or bottom of the frame (depending on whether you want the window to swing up or down) and a latch on the opposite side to lock it in place.

→ **EXTERIOR CASINGS.** If working with a sash or flange situation, remember to add exterior casings, both for

aesthetics and to seal the gap between window jamb and rough opening. Cedar is the best bet due to its rot resistance, but pine can work fine if it's primed and painted. You can use one-by-fours or rip them down for a more diminutive look. If your trim casings are also retaining the position of the sash, then there should be a minimum of ½ inch overlap. You can either miter the casings at 45° in the corners or simply cap the side casings with the head casing in a butt joint. Use 2-½-inch finish nails to install the casings.

Caulk along the top of the head casing (if on top of T-111, caulk heavily to fill the slots where the grooves run behind the casing) and down the outer edges of the side casings. For solid wood siding, and especially if the window is on the gable end with no eave protection, add a metal or wood drip edge above the head casing to run up behind the coming siding. If you opt for wood, a clapboard ripped in half works perfectly. Just run the thicker edge back to the sheathing so the siding will sit on top of it, and the thinner edge out over the window casing by up to an inch.

Finally, add the bottom casing, or apron. The apron hangs below the sill and seals the space between the sill and the siding. Cut a 1x board to length equivalent to the measurement between the outer edges of the side casings and install it.

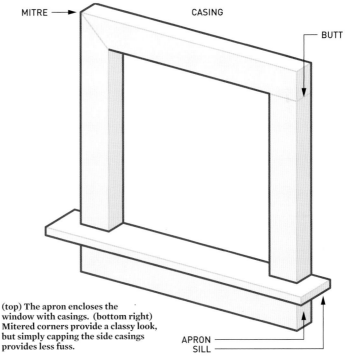

MITRE → CASING

BUTT

APRON
SILL

(top) The apron encloses the window with casings. (bottom right) Mitered corners provide a classy look, but simply capping the side casings provides less fuss.

SHED NATION CITIZEN

We are sheep farmers living on nearly 500 acres of prime pastureland in southwestern Montana. Like most working farms, this one is dotted with barns, sheds and outbuilding of various shapes and sizes. But there's one structure that stands out from the rest. It's a wood-fired sauna built of logs.

I always liked saunas and thought that perhaps I'd try building one someday. The plan got a boost when we were on a two-week canoe trip in Canada's Northwest Territories. A fierce early-winter snowstorm blew in and pinned us down on a small island. We spent four days and night in our tents, tucked in sleeping bags. As we waited out the storm, we began dreaming about how nice a hot sauna would feel. When we returned, we got to work.

The 10 x 12 building features a small front porch, two large windows and a sod roof. Inside, there's a cast-iron wood-burning stove that provides heat for the sauna.

The unusual log design we used is called cordwood construction, or stove wood

(top) A woodstove heats the sauna, and sawdust mixed into the mortar helps retain the heat. (bottom) The sauna is built utilizing cordwood construction techniques.

masonry. Instead of incorporating long logs, the walls are built of short lengths that are stacked like firewood. The spaces between the logs are filled with mortar mixed with sawdust. The sawdust acts as insulation to help retain the sauna's heat.

We built the sauna out of lodge-pole pine logs, but now think we would have been better off choosing cedar or black locust. The pine shrank more than we would've liked, but it was the only wood available at the time.

—*DAVID TYLER AND BECKY WEED, MT*

Before installing solid wood siding, or if you've already installed plywood sheet siding, next up is to trim out the tops of the walls and the corners of the shed with 1x boards. Under the eaves, install 1x material between the rafters' bird's mouths, or notch the trim under each rafter tail. If your roof was framed with trusses, depending on your roof slope, you may or may not be able to simply install trim directly

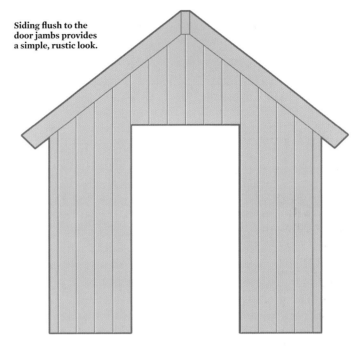

Siding flush to the door jambs provides a simple, rustic look.

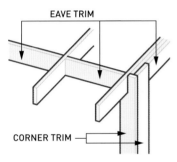

EAVE TRIM

CORNER TRIM

Depending on your rafter end detail, you may run continuous trim, or need to notch around, or stop between rafter ends.

beneath the truss rafter ends, or you may need to do some notching. Continue the trim around the corners and up under the rakes on the gable ends.

It's up to you how wide you want the corner trim to be. A 4-¼-inch dimension is common, created by making an L-shaped unit using the 3½-inch face of a one-by-four butting against the ¾-inch edge of a one-by-six ripped to 4¼ inches. For a smaller shed, you can scale down the trim to

a 3½ inch dimension by ripping a one-by-four to 2¾ and butting that into another one-by-four. Depending on your roof angle, you may need to miter one of the boards accordingly where it meets the trim on the gable end.

Though you haven't installed or even built your shed door(s), you will need to affix jambs and, in most instances, casings around these rough openings, so you can accurately run your siding. If you are using vertical siding, you may opt to forego casings around and on your door, instead running the siding flush with the jambs and using the same siding on the door itself for a uniform look.

Horizontal siding, on the other

hand, will need to be capped by trim or you will leave end grain or jagged shingle edges exposed. The process here is almost identical to the windows, except you don't need to worry about the sill, instead just running the side jambs straight down to the decking and capping the gap between the jambs and framing members with 1x trim. Leave ¼ to ½ inch of the jamb edge exposed on the door opening side so your door edge has a place to overlap the structure.

Now, before your siding goes up, take the opportunity to paint or stain your trim. See page [136] for more information on paint choices and methods.

Siding Installation

The purpose of siding is simple: protection. It protects your structure from both rain and sun, forces with the power to deteriorate and devastate all your hard work in fairly short order. Like armor, siding offers defense from the battle with Mother Nature.

Siding also provides aesthetic character. Its vertical or horizontal lines, texture, and color (or lack thereof) can make an unmistakable statement about charm, majesty, or tidiness. In general, vertical siding suggests a more casual, rustic approach (think barns and hunting cabins), while horizontal siding offers a crisp, clean, more formal look (picture beach cottages). Similarly, clapboards and shingles have a different feel than board and batten or shiplap. And wood makes a different statement than vinyl or metal.

If you plan to paint or stain your siding, consider doing it on the ground before you install it. Doing so can speed the process, and allow you to provide better coverage. See page 136 for more information.

▶ WOOD SHINGLES

Cedar shingles will naturally weather if unpainted.

Wood shingles, most often made of cedar, are the most time-consuming siding option to install, but the natural look they provide along with their effectiveness in shedding water make them a perennial favorite. The individual shingles are laid side by side in overlapping rows, with each course covering the nails in the previous course.

Pros:
- They have an incredibly long life span.
- Leaving shingles unpainted or unstained minimizes upkeep without limiting their effectiveness.
- They age naturally to a beautiful weathered gray.
- As a natural material requiring no man-ufacturing beyond sawing, they are a greener option than fabricated materials.

Cons:
- The nails used to affix shingles to the sheathing will poke through into the inside of the shed between the studs, resulting in hundreds of opportunities for injury, and hence the need to cover the interior of the shed with wallboard, a task you might ordinarily otherwise skip in a shed, unlike a house.
- They are time-consuming to install.
- Shingles are comparatively expensive.
- In some areas, wood siding can be susceptible to damage from ants or termites.

▶ INSTALLING WOOD SHINGLES

Begin with two directly overlapping courses along the base of your sheathing. Before nailing, make sure the seams between each shingle of the top course do not correspond with the seams of the course below. The second course should hang ¼ inch below the first to create a drip edge.

Nail the first course 7 inches from the bottom, and the second course 6 inches from the bottom. From this point leave a 5-inch reveal between courses.

Use zinc coated nails to minimize rust stains from forming on the shingles around each nail head.

Keeping your rows straight is critical. Snap a chalk-line to help guide you. At the ends of each course, score the shingle deeply with a utility knife and break it to fit snug against the corner board or casement trim.

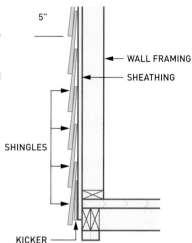

5"

WALL FRAMING

SHEATHING

SHINGLES

KICKER

Bevel siding, often called clapboards (pronounced 'clabberds') or lap siding, is made of long, thin, beveled planks—wedge-shaped with one edge thicker than the other—that run horizontally and overlap each other slightly to create a barrier from the elements.

Red cedar and spruce are the most common varieties. In some areas, clapboards and bevel siding are considered related but different, mostly with regard to length and width. Clapboards tend to run in shorter lengths of 4 to 6 feet and widths most often in the 5½- to 6-inch range, while bevel siding is generally found in longer lengths of 12 to 16 feet and widths between 8 and 10 inches. Regardless of what you call them, longer lengths (enough to span your longest wall) are indeed preferable in an effort to avoid the challenge of locating the butting ends of shorter planks directly on internal framing members (for reasons discussed above in relation to nailing shingles).

Pros:
- As with cedar shingles, they have an incredibly long life span.
- Bevel siding is quicker to install than shingles, though still requires a degree of care.
- They have an aesthetic quality that manufactured sidings try to emulate.
- As a solid wood product, it has less environmental impact than fabricated products.

Cons:
- Bevel siding is more expensive than most manufactured sidings, though cheaper than cedar shingles.
- It generally requires painting or staining every three to five years to minimize deterioration.

Bevel siding creates a crisp, clean, classic look.

Before laying any courses, snap chalk lines vertically on the sheathing to guide your nailing into the studs beneath. Depending on the width of your door, window, and corner trim and casings, double-check to see that your siding will still reach a stud, allowing for appropriate nailing. If it doesn't, you may need to add nailer studs in appropriate places.

Prior to your first course, rip a board in half and nail the thicker half along the base of your sheathing with the pointy end face up. This 'kicker' will angle your first course at a similar slant to all the remaining courses. Your first course should hang below the sheathing bottom by ¼ inch to create a drip edge. The thick edge always faces the ground, and the thin edge always points toward the roof. Make certain that it is perfectly level.

When you get to the end of the course, you'll need to cut the clapboard to length with an exact 90° cut. This is most simply and effectively accomplished with the use of a miter or chop saw, though a table saw will do the trick. Try to make it a snug fit with your trim.

The reveal you choose to show between courses is up to you, but make certain to have at least an inch of overlap between courses, and probably a bit more. If you do need to butt board ends at all, stagger them between successive courses. Unlike with shingles, your nail heads will be exposed rather than hidden by the next course. Nail about 1 to 1½ inches from the bottom (thickest) part of the siding plank, so you get a meaty chunk and are less likely to split the board. Use 2- to 2½-inch galvanized or stainless siding nails, or ring shank nails for extra holding power.

As you add successive courses, measure and mark your reveal with a speed square so you are sure to keep the courses evenly spaced and level. When you get to the top course and need to rip the board down, you can simply lay a straight edge on the board, score it with a utility knife and snap the excess off. Mitered cuts for an angled roofline can be cut with the miter saw.

For both shingles and bevel siding, keep your spacing between courses consistent from one wall to the next and on either side of a window or door opening. Variations will be noticeable.

BEVEL SIDING

PLYWOOD →

Keep your reveal consistent and even as you encircle the structure.

KICKER ——

Tongue-and-groove, shiplap barn board, and board and batten siding are all varieties of solid wood board siding. T&G and shiplap can be installed either vertically or horizontally, though horizontally provides better protection from moisture penetration. T&G siding is machined with an interlocking joint so the tongue of one board connects to the groove of the next, thereby creating a hard-to-penetrate seal. Though tongue-and-groove can ostensibly be affixed directly to the shed's studs without a sheathing layer (a material- and money-saver, though you need to factor in the additional cost of horizontal nailing members if you run vertically), having both sheathing and siding will provide additional strength.

Pros:

- Once again, solid wood siding is a natural material that minimizes environmental impacts.
- Boards install more quickly, and cost less, than shingles or bevel siding.
- Aesthetically, solid boards provide a rustic charm befitting a shed.

Cons:

- Solid wood siding is susceptible to moisture and insects, and as a result, needs to be painted or stained, with periodic maintenance.

(right) This lakeside sheds sport board-and-batten siding painted a cherry red.

→ TONGUE-AND-GROOVE.

T&G is installed simply by running successive courses up the face of the wall. Always direct the tongue edge up and the groove edge down. You can either face nail the boards into the studs using 2½-inch ring shank siding nails or blind nail at an angle through the joint where the tongue meets the board using 2½-inch finishing nails. Hide the nail head with the groove of the next course.

→ SHIPLAP BARN-BOARD.

Shiplap barn-board is a similar concept, except each board is machined with an L-shaped notch that allows it to overlap with the next. The notches can be equivalent, creating a snug fit (shiplap), or can be milled of differing widths to create a disparity in the overlap, resulting in a channel, or reveal, beneath the two boards (channel siding). In either instance, make sure the overlapping board is on top. Face nail each board into the

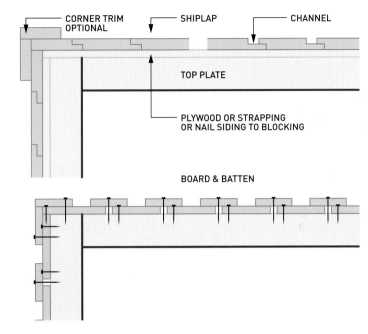

CORNER TRIM OPTIONAL — SHIPLAP — CHANNEL

TOP PLATE

PLYWOOD OR STRAPPING OR NAIL SIDING TO BLOCKING

BOARD & BATTEN

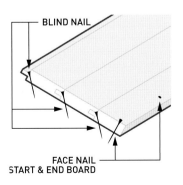

BLIND NAIL

FACE NAIL
START & END BOARD

underlying framing members about 1 to 1½ inches from the bottom of the board to effectively hold the overlapping joint closed tightly. Use 2- to 2½-inch galvanized siding nails.

→ BOARD-AND-BATTEN.

Board-and-batten siding is composed of 1x boards of two different widths alternating with one another and covering the seams between them. Using 2½-inch galvanized nails, the wide boards are nailed vertically, leaving a 1- to 2-inch gap . This gap is then covered by thinner boards (battens) that overlap the boards beneath by at least 1 inch on either side of

the gap. Use 2½- to 3-inch nails for the battens. Board-and-batten always runs vertically because the battens would collect water and quickly rot if they ran horizontally.

Note that if you want to use solid wood siding in a vertical orientation, you will need to have installed either plywood sheathing, horizontal blocking between your studs, or horizontal strapping to the exterior of the framing so that you have something into which you can drive your nails. For blocking or strapping, you'll need to know their exact placement so you can drive your nails in the correct locations.

CHAPTER 4 · DETAILS AND FINISHING

▶ NON-WOOD SIDING

The installation of non-wood siding becomes more challenging, requiring unique tools or skills.

→ **FIBER CEMENT.** Exterior fiberboard or fiber cement is a popular manufactured product made of sand, cement and cellulose fibers. It generally comes in 12-foot lengths and is produced in a variety of textures and shapes to resemble clapboards and different individual shingle styles. Installation methodology is similar to the wood products the fiberboard mimics, whether it be clapboard or shingle, though it must be cut with a carbide-tipped blade or pneumatic shears.

Pros:
- Fiberboard is assumed to have a limitless lifespan.
- It is fire-resistant, at least in comparison to wood.
- It is a durable material.
- Fiber-cement mimics wood's look, and can be painted, providing more color options than vinyl or aluminum.

Cons:
- It requires periodic repainting.
- Fiber-cement is much more expensive than vinyl, though cheaper than most solid wood products.
- Installation is challenging, and should likely be left to a professional, which adds to the cost.

→ **VINYL SIDING.** Vinyl siding panels generally come in 12½-foot lengths that mimic clapboard, though vertical panels are also available. Each panel has a nailing flange along the top and a J-shaped interlocking flange at the bottom. A lip on the nailing flange allows one panel to be hooked into the top of the panel below. Utility trim is used under sills, windows and eaves, or wherever the nailing flange has been cut off. Installing vinyl requires some special tools: a nail hole punch for punching slots in cut panels; a snap-lock punch, which allows for dimpling panels where they will meet utility panels; and an unlocking tool for separating panels. Make sure to follow the manufacturer's directions exactly.

Pros:
- Vinyl siding is relatively inexpensive, though

→ METAL SIDING. The installation of metal siding is not dissimilar from vinyl. Sheets most often come in double-wide, flat or beveled clapboard profiles with 4- or 5-inch "reveals," or in wider 8-inch wide lap-style panels. Necessary specialty tools include tin snips, double-acting shears, a steel awl, hacksaw, and a snap-lock punch tool. You may need to rent a portable brake, as well, to enable precision bending. Follow the manufacturers directions exactly and perform some extra research on the proper methodology.

Pros:
- Metal is a durable material (though susceptible to dents)
- It can be made from recycled material, and again be recycled at the end of it's life.

Cons:
- Installation is challenging for a novice.
- Color choices are limited.

professional installation adds significantly to the cost.
- It is generally considered to be maintenance-free.

Cons:
- Aesthetically, vinyl can never provide the traditional look many people desire.
- The production of vinyl is highly toxic, and it will never decompose.
- Installation is challenging for DIYers.

Building and Installing Doors

The door (or doors) to your shed should effectively keep out both the weather and critters, while simultaneously making a positive aesthetic statement, or at least not a negative one. You'll want to consider what look or style will blend with or accent your siding. And you'll need to make certain it provides a good fit, latches securely, and is sturdy.

The easiest option is to head to the nearest home improvement store and pick a pre-hung, exterior door from the rack or catalog. This works especially well if you are building a structure that is meant to mimic a home, because those are the door styles you'll find there. Also, if you intend to heat your shed space, these options might make sense due to their insulative value. Expect to pay between $150 and $500, depending on the material and style. For most sheds, though, a more rustic look is more appropriate and more cost effective. To get it, you'll want to build it yourself. And by doing so, you can custom fit it to the shed you've built.

There are a couple of door varieties and building methodologies to consider. The most common door in barn- and out-building situations is the batten door, which is made simply of vertical boards, either butting or interlocking, joined together with wood battens usually attached to the inside of the door in a combination of horizontal and diagonal runs.

If you used sheet goods for your shed's siding, you can do the same with the doors. A plywood sheet cut to size with a face frame running around its perimeter on the exterior side is simple and sturdy. Some variations on these themes are the double door, the sliding door, and the Dutch door, with its top and bottom halves hinged independently from one another.

(top) The diagonal battens work to stiffen up the whole unit. (bottom and right) Hinge hardware and finishing nails can make a bold visual statement.

→ **BATTEN DOOR.** To construct a batten door, you can use either square edged 1x, butted tightly, or for a more secure and stable door, consider utilizing V-jointed tongue-and-groove one-by-four or one-by-six cedar. First, cut the boards to length. They should run to within ³/₈ inch of the siding or trim above, and down below the top of your decking by 1 to 2 inches or to deck height if steps or ramp demand it. Measuring horizontally, the door's width should be tight to the hinged side, and the latch edge should slightly overlay the jamb. To get a proper measurement horizontally, you may need to rip one board's width.

Working on a flat surface, lay the boards down and clamp them together, but don't use glue on the joints. Then run one-by-four or one-by-six battens horizontally across the top and bottom, falling shy of the top, bottom and side edges by about 2 inches for each, and then another batten horizontally at the midpoint of the door. Attach these three battens with a bead

These batten double doors blend beautifully with the overall appearance of this shed.

A functioning latch is crucial to securing your shed from the weather and critters. Mount the hinges. Lastly, install the door pull and matching lockable latch.

cedar with construction adhesive and 3d galvanized nails. Add any additional decorative elements you'd like, such as vertical battens or an X pattern. Then add battens on the interior to add additional strength. With one-by-four cedar, make a replica face frame with the one on the exterior side, add a horizontal cross piece mid-way, and then add mitered diagonal cross battens between the horizontal rails. Again, use construction adhesive and 3d galvanized nails.

To hang a hinged door, hold the door hinges in place on the door frame and mark the mounting-hole locations. Bore pilot holes and fasten the hinges to the shed. Position the door with a ¼-inch space on the sides and top, and mark the hinge holes (a helper might be useful here). Bore pilot holes and mount the hinges.

→ **SLIDING DOOR.** A sliding door is a classic barn feature. The advantages are that it can be a bigger door than a single hinged door, there is less effort in creating a perfect fit because it hangs in front of the opening rather than within it, and it neither swings in on precious storage space nor out into the windy yard or a pile of snow that has slid off the roof and blocked its path. The downside is that

of construction adhesive and then screw them to the back of the door, being extra careful not to pop through the front of the door with your screw tips.

Finally, cut two diagonal battens running between the middle and the top and bottom battens, respectively. Miter the ends for a snug fit with the horizontal boards. Again, glue and screw them down.

If you are building double doors, attach an additional strip running vertically down and extending beyond the edge of the door. This will provide a stop, or the mating point for the two doors. Traditionally the door on the

left closes first and the right-hand door follows, stopping in place after hitting the stop strip, though flip-flopping the two will make no functional difference. Attach heavy-duty T-hinges, or something more decorative, and hang the doors in place, making certain they are level and swinging freely.

→ **PLYWOOD DOOR.** Plywood doors are an easy option. The major concern is to stiffen it and deter warping. To do so, simply cut the ply-sheet to size and add a 1x face frame around the exterior perimeter to stiffen and dress it up. Use one-by-four

it is harder to get a secure, weather-tight fit without serious effort. Also, sliding doors require enough space on the adjacent wall to have room to slide.

Sliding doors can be built exactly like swinging doors. They can be batten, plywood, or even special-ordered solid core doors.

The difference is in the hardware. You will need to purchase a sliding door track from which the door will hang and slide along on a roller assembly. There are two varieties of assemblies: one with wheels rolling in a rectangular track, the other with ball-shaped rollers running through a tube. Either

These plywood doors rely on decorative elements including the lower diagonal battens and the 45-degree top outer corners.

variety will do the trick. Follow the manufacturer's directions to properly mount the track above the door and install the rollers on the top edge of the door.

Painting or Staining Your Shed

If you've sided your shed with wood products, painting or staining its exterior will provide the final weather barrier, as well as the aesthetic exclamation point. Ideally you've been chipping away at this as you've applied trim and siding, either on the ground before assembly, or in place prior to the application of the next component. If not, it's not too late.

A successful job is dependent upon using the right paint. All coatings are specifically formulated for particular types of surfaces. Apply the incorrect kind of paint and it may quickly peel, crack or fade.

▶ PRIMERS

Plan to paint rather than staining? Begin by applying a primer. In many instances, priming the surface before you paint is the most important step of all. The job of a primer is to seal the surface so that the topcoat finish goes on smoothly, sticks well and dries evenly. Primers also hide stains, seal porous areas and create a uniform sheen across the surface. A coat of primer is critical whenever you're painting raw, unfinished surfaces or previously-painted areas that have been sanded or patched.

There are three basic types of primers: water-based latex, oil-based alkyd, and white-pigmented shellac, which is alcohol-based and primarily an interior sealer. Primer prices run from $15 to $35 per gallon.

LATEX PRIMER. Latex stain-blocking primers are the most versatile, and most can be used both indoors and outside on a wide variety of materials.

Pros:
- Latex penetrates wood well if there is moisture present.
- Latex breathes, helping to prevent the paint from peeling.
- It is flexible, allowing for expansion and contraction with humidity and temperature fluctuations.
- It cleans up with soap and water.

Con:
- Latex primer should not be covered with oil finish.

ALKYD PRIMER. Alkyd primers are excellent stain blockers that can be used indoors and out. They're often applied to raw cedar and redwood to block tannin from bleeding through the topcoat.

Pros:
- Oil resins penetrate wood more effectively than latex.
- Alkyd primers also act as an effective metal primer, coating nail heads and preventing rust.
- Oil does not raise the wood grain.
- Alkyd primer can take either oil or latex finish.

Con:
- With alkyd, you must use paint thinner to clean up your painting tools.

Exterior-grade house paints are durable, all-season coatings that are specially formulated to withstand exposure to the elements. They fall into two basic categories: latex (water-based) and alkyd (oil-based).

Exterior-grade paints come in a variety of sheens including flat, satin, semi-gloss and high gloss. Flat and satin paints are less reflective and typically are applied to house siding. Semi- and high-gloss paints usually are reserved for exterior trim work.

Nearly all major paint manufacturers produce a line of good, better and best exterior-grade paints, with prices ranging from $20 to $70 per gallon. When shopping for paint, keep in mind that price is usually a good indicator of quality. The more expensive paints contain more solids, so they produce a thicker, longer-lasting coating.

LATEX. Most painters—pros and DIYers alike—prefer latex for several reasons.

Pros:
- Latex has a relatively low odor in comparison to alkyds. Varieties low in volatile organic compounds (VOCs) provide even less odor and healthier air quality.
- It dries quickly.
- Latex cleans up easily with soap and water.

Con:
- Two coats are usually necessary to achieve satisfactory coverage.

ALKYDS. Latex might be the best choice for many home painting projects, but don't totally disregard alkyds.

Pros:
- Oil-based paints are superior stain blockers and in most cases flow on very smoothly and evenly for easy, one-coat coverage.
- They also boast exceptional adhesion and a still-wet coat of oil-based paint won't wash off the shed if it suddenly starts to rain while you're painting.

Con:
- Alkyd paints have a very pungent odor. Low-VOC options are available, but lowering VOC levels in alkyds can adversely affect the performance of the paint.
- Alkyds take a long time to dry, especially in humid weather.
- They tend to oxidize over time and become brittle, which leads to cracking and chipping.
- Lastly, the real hassle of working with solvent-based alkyds is that you must clean up with paint thinner.

▶ EXTERIOR STAINS

Penetrating stains are used to protect wood from sun and water damage without hiding its natural texture. Pigmented stains are similar to thin paints and come in various colors. Clear stains offer protection without changing the wood's color.

There are two types of exterior stains: semi-transparent and solid color. Semi-transparent stains alter the color of the wood, but let its natural texture and grain show through. They're available in wood-tone colors and several shades of gray, though more color options are beginning to surface. Solid-color stains, which are also called opaque stains, contain more pigment than the semi-transparent products. These heavy-bodied stains hide the color and grain of the wood, but not its texture. Solid-color stains are more like paints and come in a full range of colors.

Exterior stains are available in both latex- and oil-based formulations. And almost without exception, latex stains outperform oil-based stains. They last longer, fade less, and are more flexible and crack resistant. Plus, latex stains clean up with soap and water. For optimum performance, look for stain that contains 100 percent acrylic resins. Prices for exterior stains range from about $15 to $45 per gallon, but as with paints, you get what you pay for.

▶ THE AESTHETIC OPTIONS

Whichever route you take, remember that your color choices also offer a dynamic opportunity to dress-up (or down) your shed. Bold colors, or bold combinations of colors can draw attention to the structure, making a statement about its very existence. Varying trim and siding colors or setting the door apart from the rest of the structure with a strong color can add energy and even playfulness to the shed. And the simplicity of a natural wood look can be gentle and comforting. It's really just a matter of taste.

(bottom left) This bright red door adds energy and even some humor to the mix. (bottom right) This shed's green trim provides an attractive accent to the siding natural stain.

The beauty of natural wood is hard to beat.

Shelving and Storage Options

Before you start piling the yard equipment, bikes, and patio furniture inside, take a little time to create some storage opportunities. Open shelving, a workbench or potting bench, pegboards and hooks, and even a storage loft are all options worth considering.

▶ HANGING ITEMS

It's up to you how simple or detailed you choose to go with your shed, but regardless of the methodology you choose, storage and organizational opportunities abound, with the only limit being one's own creative impulses.

Pegboards, along with compatible hooks and hanging devices, can be purchased at most any home improvement center. They can be hung above a workbench or potting bench for easy accessibility to tools and gardening equipment, or on any available wall space.

Another option is a store bought wire-rack shelving system. A 5 to 6 inch-deep shelf with wrap-around retaining fencing will keep cleaning supplies, containers of paint thinner, or other small items securely stowed. These can even be affixed to the inside of the shed door, to really maximize space.

Purchase J-hooks, S-hooks, utility hooks or ladder hooks from your local hardware store to hang bicycles, ladders, or other tools from ceiling joists. And of course, the simplest hanging methodology is simply to drive some nails into studs to hang shovels, loppers, hammers, and virtually any other garden or workshop hand tools.

(top) Ample storage space can be discovered in the rafters for less-needed items, lumber, or off-season equipment. (bottom) Place tools and other often-used equipment on hooks on the wall for easy access.

Keeping in mind that you are fitting out a shed rather than a custom kitchen, shelving units can be as simple as pine one-by-eights, one-by-tens, or one-by-twelves (or ¾-inch plywood ripped to the appropriate depth) supported by cleats made of two-by-fours ripped in half and screwed to successive studs with 2½-inch-long screws. Fasten the shelving to the cleats from above with 1½-inch screws. If you are concerned about items falling behind the shelf in the gaps between the studs, you can add a one-by-four retaining wall, or backsplash.

For maximum strength, your shelves should run from wall to wall, so there will be cleats supporting the shelf on three sides. If you can only run partway along a wall, you may need to add a brace below the unsupported corner.

Make 45° miter cuts on a two-by-four so that it is positioned vertically. Run the bottom miter off the side of a framing member.

Screw through the brace into the wall stud with 2½-inch screws. The upper end should rest flush on the underside of the shelf, at least two-thirds of the way to the board's outer edge.

Screw the shelf down into the miter cut end grain with two 1½-inch screws.

You may opt to add a brace to a very long and fairly wide shelf even if it spans from wall to wall. A brace midway can add needed stability and prevent sagging.

You can stack numerous shelves one above the next, but don't crowd them too much or you won't leave enough vertical space for the items you intend to store. A good rule of thumb is to leave between 12 and 16 inches from one shelf to the next. The gap between the lower shelves is often bigger than the gap between the upper shelves because bigger, heavier items tend to be stored lower so they don't have to be hoisted.

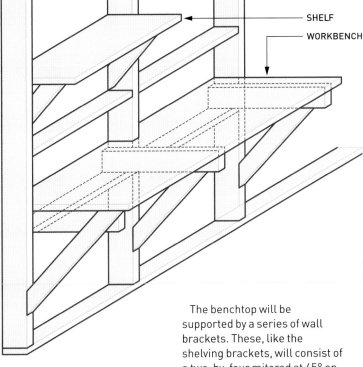

SHELF

WORKBENCH

Simple mitered two by fours easily support a shelf and its contents. For a workbench extra bracing provides additional strength.

If you intend to use your shed for any type of active work, whether it be related to gardening, equipment repair and maintenance, or woodworking, a sturdy workbench is essential.

Make your benchtop from ¾-inch plywood (ACX ply will provide a smooth work surface) ripped and cut to the appropriate dimensions. The bench's depth is dependent on the amount of workspace you envision needing as well as the size of the shed (a 3-foot-deep bench in a 4-foot-deep shed will surely make life challenging).

The benchtop will be supported by a series of wall brackets. These, like the shelving brackets, will consist of a two-by-four mitered at 45° on each end, run off the front edge of the framing members below. In this case, you'll also add an additional brace to add strength and stability: a horizontal two-by-four running from the sheathing, directly along the underside of the bench top, and attached to the side at the diagonal support brace.

Use 2½-inch screws to fasten both the diagonal and horizontal brace members to the side of the framing stud. A typical bench top is 36 inches above the floor, though you can adjust that up or down slightly depending on

what is comfortable for those who will be utilizing it. Take extra care to make sure the top of each bracket is level as you attach them to the studs.

You'll need a brace at each end of the bench and an additional brace for every 16 inches of length beyond 32 inches, spacing them appropriately. Screw the benchtop down onto the brackets with 1½-inch screws. You can either notch the bench top around each stud or run it along the front of the studs and add a one-by-four retaining wall along the back edge of the bench, fastening it to the stud faces.

If your bench is on a gable-end wall and therefore has some wall space above it, consider hanging a pegboard here, or on another wall that affords the space. These are great for hanging tools and gardening equipment.

▶ ADDING LOFT STORAGE

Depending on your roof height, you may have the opportunity to make use of the space above your shed's ceiling joists. This is valuable real estate and can be well-utilized for less-needed items, lumber, or off-season equipment.

An easy method of creating a loft is to simply span a couple of joist bays with ¾-inch plywood or 1x boards and fasten them down to the joists with 1½-inch screws. Run the decking lengthwise to straddle several ceiling joists. And as with your floor decking, make

certain to have butt joints (if you have any) meet midway on the joist.

To prevent items from rolling or falling off over the loft edge, affix a two-by-six or two-by-eight to the outside of the lead ceiling joist so that it stands proud of the joist, creating a 2- to 4-inch-tall retaining wall.

Access to the loft can take on several forms, from the basic to the elaborate. For simplicity's sake, use one of the stepladders that you'll likely be storing in the shed as your means to access

the loft. For a more permanent solution, build a simple ladder utilizing two-by-fours for the ladder's legs and two-by-threes for the rungs. Place the bottom and top rungs 8 inches from the ladder ends, and run the intermediate rungs every 16 inches. Affix the rungs by cutting 1-inch-deep by 1½-inch-tall notches in each leg at the appropriate intervals, using a circular saw to cut numerous kerfs and then chiseling out the remains. Assuming your joists are 24 inches o.c., cut your rungs 19 inches in length. Add wood glue to each notch before inserting the rungs, and then screw them in place from the outside of the uprights with coarse-threaded 2½-inch screws.

If your shed is wide enough to accommodate the ladder horizontally, consider adding hinges to the top of the uprights and attaching them to the wall top plate on one side of the shed.

If you intend to store heavy equipment in the loft, consider fortifying your loft decking with a second layer of plywood, or by building with two-by-six joists instead of two-by-fours. You might also consider installing a pulley system for hoisting and lowering items. And if you're going to this effort, consider building the rough opening to fit an attic-type, fold-down staircase that hinges with spring-loaded brackets.

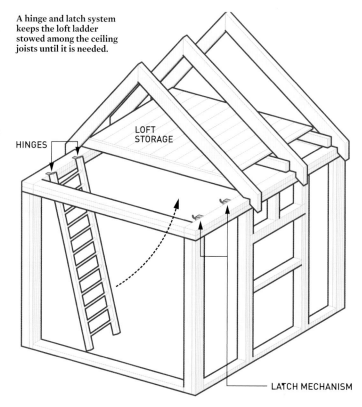

A hinge and latch system keeps the loft ladder stowed among the ceiling joists until it is needed.

HINGES

LOFT STORAGE

LATCH MECHANISM

CHAPTER 7

Shed Plans

A shed can be many things to many people. Here are some different designs, unique materials, and creative functions to help you imagine your perfect shed.

Small is Beautiful

$1,000-$2,000

This modest 6 × 8 foot shed is big enough for a variety of tools, but not so large that it dominates a backyard landscape. The straightforward design is easy to expand—up to about 8 × 12—to suit your storage needs. It utilizes standard framing techniques and materials, and is sheathed with ½-inch plywood and sided with one-by-six tongue-and-groove cedar boards. The exterior trim is rough-sawn cedar. Materials for this shed should cost between $1000 and $2000.

▶ BUILDING THE FLOOR

Begin by clearing and leveling your site, and marking out the building's location. Find the highest corner of the site and excavate for the first foundation corner block. Add 2- to 3-inches of crushed stone. Then excavate and prepare the three other corners, lay your blocks and work to level them with one another.

The deck frame utilizes double-wide front and back band joists, sandwiching single-width side band joists. Cut two-by-six stock to length for the front and back rim joists, and then lay out

the locations of the floor joists on 16-inch centers. Nail joist hangers to the inside surface of each inner joist using 1½-inch joist hanger nails. Next, place the inner front and back joists between the corner blocks, and then cut and position the floor joists. Nail the joists in place, then attach the side band joists and then the outer joists to the front and back of the floor frame.

Compare opposite diagonal measurements of the floor assembly to check that it's square, and nail ¾-inch plywood to the joists from the shed floor.

Cut two-by-six stock to size for the door and window headers. Use pieces of ½-inch plywood as spacers between the two-by-sixes to bring the header assemblies to 2½ inches thick. Nail together the header pieces with 16d common nails.

Cut two-by-four stock to length for the wall studs and window and door jack studs. Nail each jack stud to a wall stud with 8d common nails. Build the four corner posts by nailing three two-by-four spacers between two studs as shown on page 80.

Begin framing the back wall by laying out the stud locations on the top and bottom plates. Then, lay out the framing member on the deck. Nail through the top plate and into the wall members, then secure the bottom plate. Frame the window opening and nail the second top plate to the wall, keeping its ends back 3½ inches from each end of the wall.

Check for squareness, and then apply ½-inch plywood sheathing.

Stand the rear wall, bracing it with two-by-fours nailed between the wall and the outside floor joists. Nail the bottom plate to the deck so the plywood sheathing is flush with the edge of the deck. Frame the front wall, but don't apply the sheathing yet. Instead, stand the framed wall and brace it. Position the wall ½ inch from the deck edges to allow for the thickness of the sheathing.

Then frame the side walls, one at a time, and stand them. Leave the second top plate off the side walls until they are raised. Nail the walls together at the corners, and then cut and install the side wall top plates. Apply the remaining plywood sheathing. At the side walls, keep the plywood 1½ inches down from the top to provide room to nail the gable-end sheathing.

▶ FRAMING THE ROOF

The roof is a gentle 5 in 12 pitch. It uses standard rafters, but because of the gentle pitch and the diminutive size, you can replace ceiling joists and a ridge beam with simple plywood gussets joining each rafter pair at the ridge.

Use a framing square to lay out the 5 in 12 pitch of the first roof rafter. Cut out the rafter and use it as a pattern to make the second rafter. Test the first two for proper fit, then trace and cut the remaining rafters.

Cut a gusset for each truss from ½-inch-thick plywood and nail it to the rafters with 1½-inch roofing nails. Toenail the trusses to the front and rear walls with 8d common nails. At the gable ends, keep the gussets on the inside faces of the trusses. There will be no rake overhang to build out.

Cut two-by-six stock to length for the subfascia and nail the boards to the rafter ends with 16d common nails. Cut and install the gable-

end sheathing, and then nail one-by-six pine furring over the gable rafters. Then install the cedar fascia and rake trim. Install the plywood roof deck, allowing it to overhang the fascia by ½ inch along the eaves. Nail aluminum drip edge to the eaves, apply roofing felt, and then install your asphalt roof shingles. Or if you choose to use cedar roofing, run skip sheathing across the rafters and then your courses of shingles or shakes.

▶ INSTALLING SIDING, WINDOWS AND DOORS

Since tongue-and-groove siding is installed vertically, add two-by-four blocks between the studs, about halfway up the wall. Cut and install these nailers by toenailing them between adjacent studs. Cut siding boards to length and begin installing them at a corner of the building. Face nail the first board, but fasten succeeding boards with nails driven diagonally through

the tongue so the heads will be hidden.

After painting or staining the siding, install the door and window jambs. At the windows, slope or miter the sill pieces about 5° toward the outside of the building. Use 1x cedar stock to create inner and outer stops to hold the barn sash windows in place. Rip door and window trim and shed corner boards from

rough-sawn cedar. Cut each piece to length and nail in place.

Cut siding boards to length for the shed door. Use clamps to pull the boards together, but don't glue the joints. Cut the battens for the door, and screw them to the inside surface of the boards. Install the door and hardware. Then, stain or paint the windows, door, and remaining trim.

GARDEN SHED

7'5" DEEP X 8'3" WIDE X 9'4" HIGH

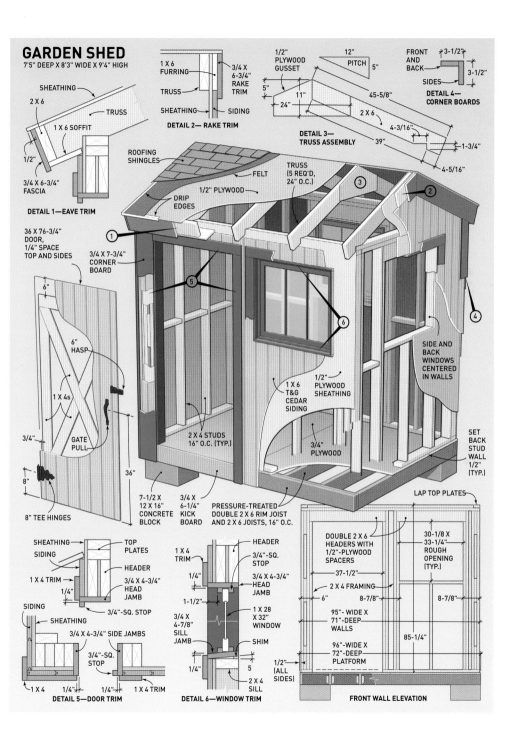

DETAIL 1—EAVE TRIM

SHEATHING
2 X 6
TRUSS
1 X 6 SOFFIT
1/2"
3/4 X 6-3/4"
FASCIA

DETAIL 2— RAKE TRIM

1 X 6 FURRING
TRUSS
SHEATHING
3/4 X 6-3/4" RAKE TRIM
SIDING

DETAIL 3— TRUSS ASSEMBLY

1/2" PLYWOOD GUSSET
12" PITCH 5"
5"
11"
24"
45-5/8"
2 X 6
4-3/16"
39"
1-3/4"
4-5/16"

DETAIL 4— CORNER BOARDS

FRONT AND BACK
3-1/2"
3-1/2"
SIDES

ROOFING SHINGLES
DRIP EDGES
FELT
1/2" PLYWOOD
TRUSS (5 REQ'D, 24" O.C.)

36 X 76-3/4" DOOR, 1/4" SPACE TOP AND SIDES
3/4 X 7-3/4" CORNER BOARD

6"
6" HASP
1 X 4s
GATE PULL
3/4"
8"
8" TEE HINGES
36"

SIDE AND BACK WINDOWS CENTERED IN WALLS

1 X 6 T&G CEDAR SIDING
1/2" PLYWOOD SHEATHING
2 X 4 STUDS 16" O.C. (TYP.)
3/4" PLYWOOD

SET BACK STUD WALL 1/2" (TYP.)

7-1/2 X 12 X 16" CONCRETE BLOCK
3/4 X 6-1/4" KICK BOARD
PRESSURE-TREATED DOUBLE 2 X 6 RIM JOIST AND 2 X 6 JOISTS, 16" O.C.

LAP TOP PLATES

DETAIL 5—DOOR TRIM

SHEATHING
SIDING
TOP PLATES
HEADER
1 X 4 TRIM
3/4 X 4-3/4" HEAD JAMB
1/4"
3/4"-SQ. STOP
SIDING
SHEATHING
3/4 X 4-3/4" SIDE JAMBS
3/4"-SQ. STOP
1 X 4
1/4"
1/4"
1 X 4 TRIM

DETAIL 6—WINDOW TRIM

HEADER
1 X 4 TRIM
3/4"-SQ. STOP
3/4 X 4-3/4" HEAD JAMB
1/4"
1-1/2"
1 X 28 X 32" WINDOW
3/4 X 4-7/8" SILL JAMB
SHIM
1/4"
5
2 X 4 SILL

FRONT WALL ELEVATION

DOUBLE 2 X 6 HEADERS WITH 1/2"-PLYWOOD SPACERS
30-1/8 X 33-1/4" ROUGH OPENING (TYP.)
37-1/2"
2 X 4 FRAMING
6"
8-7/8"
8-7/8"
95"- WIDE X 71"-DEEP WALLS
85-1/4"
96"-WIDE X 72"-DEEP PLATFORM
1/2" (ALL SIDES)

155

Groundskeeper

$2,500-$3,500

This basic 9 x 13-foot shed is a good project for first-timers, as it uses conventional framing methods very much in keeping with those described in this book, and its use of T-111 for the siding and doors speeds the building process along. Materials costs should be in the $2500 to $3500 range.

Start by laying out and staking the four corners of the shed. Dig 6-inch-deep depressions at each corner and at the center of each long wall. Pour about 4 inches of crushed rock into each depression, level it and compact the rock with a hand tamper.

▶ BUILDING THE FLOOR

Cut pressure-treated two-by-six sill lumber to lie flush with the outer edges of the blocks, and then cut the band joists that rest on top of the sill. Stagger the sill and band-joist lumber at the corners and nail each sill piece to the bottom of a band joist. Fit the offset corners together and secure them with 16d galvanized nails. Cut two-by-six joists to fit between the band joists. Then install ¾-inch tongue-and-groove plywood flooring.

Conventional framing methods, a spacious layout, and crisp, no-frills design make this a great option for a beginning DIYer.

▶ ADDING THE WALLS

Cut the wall plates for the long walls and lay out the studs on 16-inch centers. At both ends of each wall, install triple studs to act as nailers for the short walls. For the wall with the door, mark its rough opening on the plates. Build a door header from two-by-sixes sandwiched around a ½-inch plywood spacer. The length of the header is the rough opening plus 3 inches for the jack studs. Cut two jack studs to the height of the rough opening and nail those to kings posts. Then nail the header in place and add the second top plate.

To add the siding, cut a sheet of T-111 to length, set it flush with the top plate, and nail it every 6 inches along the edges and every 10 inches elsewhere with 8d nails. Install the remaining sheets in like fashion. Tip the wall up, plumb it and have a helper secure it with braces. Nail through the sole plate with 16d nails, as well as through the siding into the band joist and sill. Then build the opposite long wall.

On the window wall, you can space the studs from a center stud to suit the window openings. Plan the short, cripple studs that are above and below the openings to fall on 16-inch centers. Secure your king, jack and cripple studs, to the plates and then install your headers and sills. Install the siding but leave the second top plate off each end wall until they're up.

You can install the windows while the wall is still on the ground. Then raise the walls and nail them at the corners. Finally, add a top plate onto each end wall so it overlaps the lower top plate on the long walls.

▶ FRAMING THE ROOF

The roof utilizes trusses that can be assembled on the shed floor or another piece of plywood. For this 7 in 12 pitch, use two-by-fours to make your bottom chords and trusses, and tie them together with ½-inch plywood gussets. The inner trusses are simple triangles, but the end trusses have vertical nailers for securing the siding. After lifting and securing the trusses, install siding on the gable ends and build the gable overhang from two-by-four blocking nailed along the rake of the roof. Cover the blocking with one-by-six cedar boards.

Deck the roof with ½-inch plywood and cover it with roofing felt and install asphalt shingles or metal roofing. Finally, build a door with a sheet of T-111 and use 1x material to stiffen it up.

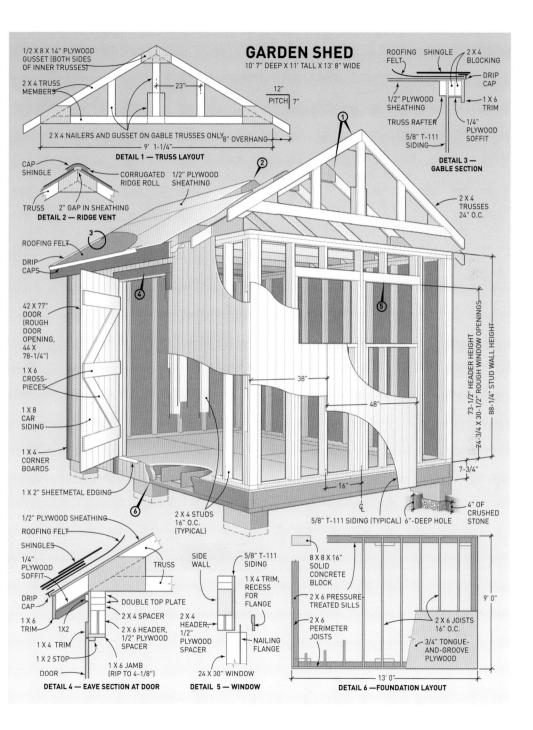

The Big Red Shed

$3,500-$4,500

Here's a handsome Colonial-style storage shed that's versatile and well-designed. In fact, it's really two sheds in one: a 10 × 12 foot toolshed for general storage and an 8 × 10 foot open-bay extension that's ideal for keeping firewood stacked and dry.

The floor could be either a concrete slab or a wood frame assembly on solid concrete blocks or pressure-treated six-by-six skids. If you go with the slab, it's a good idea to hire an excavator and mason to have the job done right. Materials for this shed, not including foundation work, will cost between $3500 and $4500.

▶ FRAMING THE WALLS

Unlike a typical wall with vertical studs, the walls in this structure have long horizontal two-by-four purlins that provide nailing support for the vertical siding. In place of the vertical studs are short two-by-four blocking members. Start by building the front and rear walls of the main shed. If you're building on a slab, use pressure-treated lumber for the bottom plates.

Frame the front wall to accommodate the door and windows. The rear wall has no openings, leaving plenty of wall space for hanging tools and installing shelves.

With the wall frames flat on the floor, check that they're square by measuring the diagonals. Add diagonal metal wall bracing to the main shed's walls to increase frame stiffness. Attach tongue-and-groove cedar siding to the horizontal two-by-fours with 2½-inch ring-shank siding nails. If you're on a slab, bore holes corresponding to the anchor bolts in the bottom wall plates.

Tilt up the walls, set them over the bolts, and secure the walls with washers and nuts. Plumb the walls and temporarily brace them with two-by-fours fastened to stakes driven into the ground. Frame the two gable-end walls, raise them between the front and rear walls, and nail the corners together. Then add the cedar siding. Build the extension in the same way, but use a full-length double two-by-six header to span the wide opening.

Take care of all your outdoor storage needs with this two-for-one backyard building.

▶ FRAMING THE ROOF

Make use of the open floor space as a platform for building the roof trusses. Each truss consists of a pair of two-by-four rafters and a two-by-four chord that also acts as a ceiling joist. At the corners are plywood gussets secured with construction adhesive and roofing nails.

Note that the gable trusses have collar ties so there's extra wood to which you can nail the siding. When you build the gable trusses, add flat two-by-four pieces, or shoes, to their bottom chords so the gables can be set slightly proud of the walls below them.

The roof has a 10 in 12 pitch. This creates 50° angles at the rafter and chord ends. Nail the gable trusses to the main shed first. Place the remaining trusses over the vertical blocking, secure them with screws, and install the plywood deck and shingles.

At the extension, set a gable truss in place against the main shed wall. With the trusses and decking in place, sheathe the structure with one-by-six tongue-and-groove cedar siding. The roof is covered with slate-gray, architectural-style asphalt shingles, though metal roofing could also be utilized. The main shed has three tilt-in barn-sash windows and a door that's made from the same tongue-and-groove one-by-six cedar used for the siding. Complete the job by nailing on the window trim and corner boards.

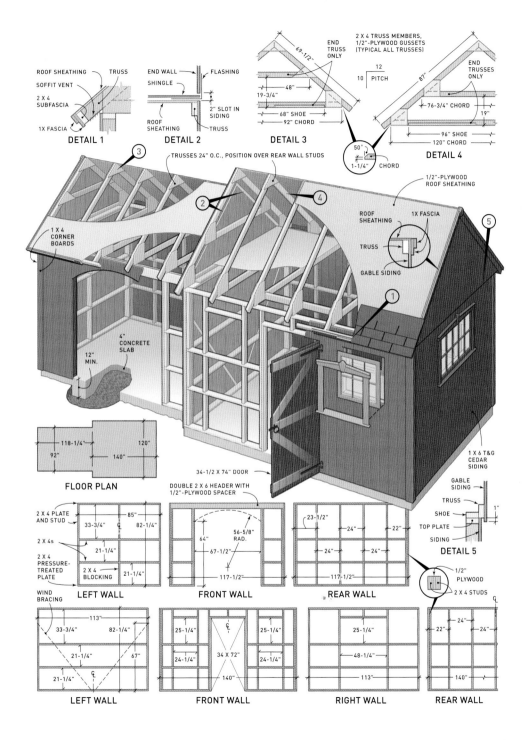

Shed Reckoning

$4,000-$5,000

This handsome Colonial-style garden shed is proof that form and function can coexist in a backyard building. It isn't just practical, spacious and sturdy. It's also beautifully designed to be an asset—not an eyesore.

The 12 × 16 foot building has easy to install one-by-six vertical cedar siding. There are two pairs of double doors, three tilt-in barn-sash windows, and a transom window over the gable-end doors. The roof is covered with architectural-style asphalt shingles and a continuous ridge vent.

The interior of the shed is divided into a 12 × 12 foot space intended for general storage and a 4 × 12 foot potting area. Overhead, you can add a small loft for storing seasonal items. Expect to pay between $4000 and $5000 for materials.

▶ FLOOR FRAME DETAILS

The shed is supported on solid concrete blocks laid out in three rows and placed directly on the ground. If the building site isn't flat, level the earth or stack two or more blocks as required.

Build the floor frame by placing three two-by-eight mudsills on top of the rows of blocks, and then lay two-by-six joists across the sills. Space the joists 16 inches on center and nail them to two-by-six perimeter band joists. For the shed floor, use ¾-inch tongue-and-groove ACX plywood, fastened to the joists with 8d galvanized nails.

This stylish, multipurpose outbuilding utilizes some decorative trim and architectural accents to make a strong aesthetic statement.

These shed walls have horizontal purlins that provide nailing support for the siding, rather than typical vertical studs. Build the two long walls first. Frame the front wall to accommodate a 58-inch-wide door opening and two 24 × 36 inch windows. Nail the top and bottom wall plates to the end studs. Then install the long purlins, followed by the vertical blocking.

With the walls flat on the floor, install the siding with 2½-inch ring-shank siding nails. Tilt up the walls and fasten them with 3-inch-long deck screws. Temporarily hold each wall upright with a diagonal two-by-four brace.

Build the two gable-end walls, framing one with a 58-inch-wide door opening, a 24-inch square window and a 10 × 59 inch transom window. Install the siding, and raise the gable-end walls between the front and rear walls.

The roof is framed with nine trusses that are assembled on the floor. Each roof truss is made up of a pair of two-by-four rafters and a two-by-six bottom chord. Cut one end of each rafter to 40°; they will form a 10 in 12 roof slope when joined together at the peak. Fasten together the three boards that make up each truss, securing ½-inch plywood gussets at the corners with construction adhesive and 1½-inch roofing nails.

First install the two gable-end trusses. Then place each standard truss directly over a line of vertical blocking. Drive a screw up through the underside of the top plate and into the bottom chord. Cover the trusses with ½-inch CDX plywood and install the shingles. Finish up by building and hanging the batten doors, which are made from the same one-by-six cedar used for the siding. Then nail on the window trim and install the barn-sash windows.

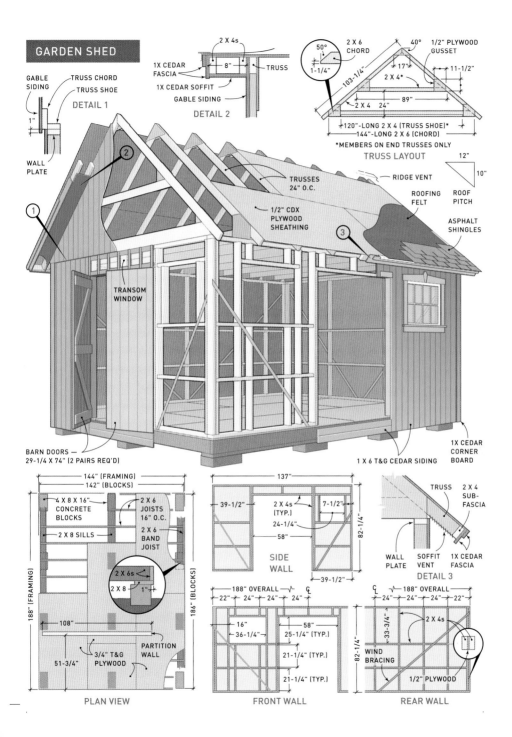

GARDEN SHED

DETAIL 1

GABLE SIDING
TRUSS CHORD
TRUSS SHOE
TRUSS SHOE
WALL PLATE
1"

DETAIL 2

2 X 4s
1X CEDAR FASCIA
8"
TRUSS
1X CEDAR SOFFIT
GABLE SIDING

TRUSS LAYOUT

2 X 6 CHORD
40°
1/2" PLYWOOD GUSSET
50°
1-1/4"
17"
11-1/2"
103-1/4"
2 X 4*
2 X 4   24"
89"
2 X 6   120"-LONG 2 X 4 (TRUSS SHOE)*
144"-LONG 2 X 6 (CHORD)
*MEMBERS ON END TRUSSES ONLY

12"
10"
ROOF PITCH

TRUSSES 24" O.C.
RIDGE VENT
1/2" CDX PLYWOOD SHEATHING
ROOFING FELT
ASPHALT SHINGLES
TRANSOM WINDOW
BARN DOORS — 29-1/4 X 74" (2 PAIRS REQ'D)
1 X 6 T&G CEDAR SIDING
1X CEDAR CORNER BOARD

PLAN VIEW

144" (FRAMING)
142" (BLOCKS)
4 X 8 X 16" CONCRETE BLOCKS
2 X 6 JOISTS 16" O.C.
2 X 8 SILLS
2 X 6 BAND JOIST
2 X 6s
2 X 8   1"
188" (FRAMING)
186" (BLOCKS)
108"
51-3/4"
3/4" T&G PLYWOOD
PARTITION WALL

SIDE WALL

137"
39-1/2"
2 X 4s (TYP.)
7-1/2"
24-1/4"
58"
82-1/4"
39-1/2"

DETAIL 3

TRUSS   2 X 4 SUB-FASCIA
WALL PLATE   SOFFIT VENT   1X CEDAR FASCIA

FRONT WALL

188" OVERALL
22"   24"   24"   24"
16"
36-1/4"
58"
25-1/4" (TYP.)
21-1/4" (TYP.)
21-1/4" (TYP.)
82-1/4"

REAR WALL

188" OVERALL
24"   24"   24"   22"
33-3/4"
2 X 4s
WIND BRACING
1/2" PLYWOOD

Build Your Own Greenhouse

If a seed-starter shed isn't enough to satisfy your gardening green thumb, consider a full greenhouse. You can buy kit greenhouses in various shapes and sizes. When function outweighs aesthetics, look to the utilitarian hoop houses that can enclose large spaces at low cost. Most greenhouse models, however, are rectangular with either rounded or angled eaves, ridgepoles and low- to medium-pitched roofs.

Wood and heavy-gauge aluminum greenhouses glazed with glass or multi-wall polycarbonate cost two to three times as much as light-gauge aluminum, PVC, or steel tube frames glazed either with thin-mil polycarbonate or polyethylene. Most kit prices do not include greenhouse equipment or the cost of the foundation. The kit designation usually means just the frame, panels, and hardware. Expect to pay between $25 and $50 per square foot for a wood or heavy-gauge aluminum structure glazed with glass or a multiwall polycarbonate.

▶ INSTALLING THE FOUNDATION

Many small greenhouses do not require a permanent foundation, but check with your town's building department. For upwards of 50 square feet, you'll most likely need a foundation of some sort. Pouring 8-inch diameter concrete piers below the frost line beneath each corner of the structure is the most cost-effective means. Removing the sod from the building's footprint and laying a gravel base provides an easy-to-maintain floor surface. Then lay pressure treated timbers from pier to pier around the perimeter. For a smaller unit, one course of four-by-fours or four-by-sixes will be sufficient, but for a larger structure, consider doubling them up and joining them with lagbolts and washers.

Build a kit greenhouse and have a big-league growing season.

This end-wall frame utilized the same system as a wood-built shed frame.

GREENHOUSE SOURCE LIST

B.C. GREENHOUSE BUILDERS LTD. *(www.bcgreenhouses.com, 888-391-4433).* Offers a wide selection of styles and sizes, some with curved eaves or decorative tops. Kits include heavy-duty aluminum frames and panels of single-pane glass, double-pane glass, double-wall polycarbonate or triple-wall polycarbonate. Prices range from under $2000 to about $8000 for standard models, depending upon size and glazing options.

EASYGROW GREENHOUSES. *(www.easygrow.com, 800-959-3649).* Specializes in a gambrel-roof greenhouse with twin-walled polycarbonate panels, six roof vents and gutters. Sizes range from 7 x 9 to 8 x 16. Seven-year warranty offers peace of mind. Priced from $1400 to $3000.

GOTHIC ARCH GREENHOUSES. *(www.gothicarchgreen houses.com, 800-531-4769).* Models have a unique arched design with heart cypress frames and a choice of corrugated fiberglass, corrugated polycarbonate or 8mm double-wall polycarbonate for the panels. Prices range from $1600 to $4000, and a 10-year warranty covers everything but the fiberglass.

RION GREENHOUSES. *(www.riongreenhousekit. com, 866-448-8229).* Frame is constructed of resin PVC that snaps together with no tools and holds 4mm double-wall polycarbonate panels. Available in several different lengths and widths, all with the same barn-style roof. Prices range from $1400 to $3000.

SUNSHINE GARDENHOUSE *(www.gardenhouse.com, 888-272-9333).* Features redwood frames and 4mm double-wall, polycarbonate panels. Panels come preinstalled in frame for easy assembly. Prices range from $1200 to $4000.

The ridge beam goes into place.

▶ BUILDING THE FRAME

Each kit is different, but in general, assembling a greenhouse is not that different from assembling a wood-framed shed. The walls will have top and bottom plates and vertical studs, and the roof will have rafters and a ridge beam.

Assemble each wall flat on the ground, bolting together the various pieces according the kit plans. Use a nut driver or a socket wrench to make sure all the fasteners are tight. With a helper, walk one of the side walls into place on the

foundation timbers, and screw the bottom wall plate to the foundation. Brace the wall in its vertical position as you install the adjacent gable-end walls, and bolt them together. Then add the fourth wall.

With your helpers, join the gable ends together by lifting the ridge beam into place and bolting it to the peaks of the gable-end walls.

Before running the rafters from top plate to ridge beam, apply self-sticking weatherstripping to seal the roof panels. Some greenhouses may use horizontal

purlins to provide extra support for the rafters.

Install the roof panels first. The glazing will be held in place with a metal strip that gets screwed to the frame. Don't over-tighten the fasteners or you run the risk of cracking the glass. Run the screws down until snug with a drill or driver, then tighten an additional quarter-turn by hand with a screwdriver. On the walls, apply the self-sticking foam tape to all the glazing channels, then put the glazing in place and screw the unit down to the framing.

Built for Neverland

If the kids are clamoring for a backyard playhouse, virtually any shed-like structure can adequately fit the bill. But if you are looking to create something magical, nothing does the job like a playhouse in the trees. Treehouses capture the imagination of kids and adults alike with their whimsy and precarious positioning amidst the limbs and branches.

This elevated playland would do Peter Pan proud. The core is a cockeyed treehouse that's been squeezed through Alice's looking glass. Hardly a right angle can be found on the 7 × 6 foot structure. The roof tilts this way, the windows bend that way, and the chimney makes a dogleg left, then right.

Adventurers can approach the treehouse on two swinging bridges strung from nearby trees. Two strands of 3/8-inch galvanized aircraft cable undergird each bridge, to which wooden brackets and planking are attached. Other features include a cargo net kids can jump into, a suspension bridge to a fort, a slide made of slick aluminum siding, and a 130-foot-long zip line with an attached swing seat.

Treehouses can be a lot simpler than this one. But even a basic platform with railings and a ladder requires a degree of knowledge and creative problem-solving that quickly moves beyond the realm of shed-building. The first concern is to understand the trees you might be working with.

Some species are better than others. Beech, fir, maple, ash, and oak are deep-rooted and their wood is strong. On the other end of the spectrum, birch, buckeye, cottonwood, willow, and poplar are weaker or shorter-lived. For a single-tree structure, the ideal candidate would have a 30-40 inch diameter.

Decay is the enemy when it comes to deciding where to build. Avoid trees laden with fungus or moss. Tap with a mallet to listen for a dampened sound, which indicates rot. A broad root system is good. Still unsure? Many arborists will check a tree for free or for a small price.

Once you've determined where to build, you need to determine what to build. The sky is the limit, but as you design, remember that building 20 or even 10 feet off the ground is decidedly more challenging than building on the ground. So don't push beyond the reality of your skills.

Many carpentry rules were thrown to the wind in building this cockeyed treehouse.

TREEHOUSE BUILDING RESOURCES

TREEHOUSE WORKSHOP, SEATTLE, WA.
(www.treehouseworkshop. com, 206-782-0208). Offers a design service for those who want to build their own tree house, phone or on-site consulting services, and treehouse construction workshops.

YESTERMORROW DESIGN/BUILD SCHOOL, WARREN, VT.
(www.yestermorrow.org, 888-496-5541). Offers a seven-day sustainable treehouse design & construction course and a two-day treehouse design workshop.

THE NORTHWEST TREEHOUSE SCHOOL, FALL CITY, WA .
(www.nwtreehouseschool. com, 206-782-0208). Provides three-day treehouse construction workshops, focusing on platform mechanics and construction.

▶ TOOLS OF THE TREEHOUSE TRADE

How you attach your treehouse to the tree is a critical determinant for both the structure's durability and the tree's long-lasting health. A treehouse focuses its entire weight onto a few points, so those attachments need to be bombproof. Nails won't cut it. And when multiple branches or trees support the foundation, joints must be flexible to allow for tree sway.

You're likely to find some specific fastening hardware in the toolbox of the professional treehouse builder (yes, there are professionals). Galvanized lagscrews (¼-inch diameter, and about 4 to 6 inches long) and a washer provide a solid union between tree and joist. Trees react badly to two closely spaced puncture wounds, with the space between rotting out; use a single large bolt instead.

Garnier Limbs are 1¼-inch-thick tree anchor bolts designed specifically for the purpose of creating a "limb" where one is needed. They have threaded rod on one end that is screwed into the tree, a flange (or collar) in the middle that rests against the tree, and an unthreaded anchor that juts out, acting as the limb that will support the load—up to 8,000 pounds worth. A variety of metal poles and brackets can fit the protruding anchor.

Cables can be used to support overhanging platforms and to create suspension systems. The cables are anchored with eyebolts, and turnbuckles allow you to adjust the tension. A variety of bracket designs allow beams to move slightly, to keep a tree's swaying (and growth) from pulling apart the structure.

Lagscrew, garnier limb, cabled support, and flexible joints

What goes up can come down—including you. Here are a few tips to avoid a smashed drill, or worse, when the job site is high in a tree.

Rent scaffolding, at least to build the platform. Ladders plus round trunks can lead to disaster. Wear a climbing harness. A model made for tree work will be more comfortable, but a rock-climbing harness will do. Create a convenient safety system by tying lengths of "static" climbing rope or nylon webbing to the tree at various points. As you move about, unclip from one anchor and clip into another using locking carabiners.

But a harness isn't enough. This is dangerous work—don't try it until you've done your homework in safety and technique. Take a climbing class to learn knots and ropework. Wear a hard hat. And never work alone.

Hang tools in five-gallon buckets with rope from nearby branches to avoid dropping them—a major inconvenience. Put pencils on a string leash. Hoisting heavy beams requires a block-and-tackle setup.

A Garden Folly

A folly in the architectural realm is a building of eccentric or over-elaborate design, usually built for decorative rather than practical purposes. The construction of this garden folly was an educational tool for a group of students learning to build with natural materials during a program at the Yestermorrow Design/Build School.

NATURAL BUILDING RESOURCES

YESTERMORROW DESIGN/BUILD SCHOOL, WARREN, VT. *(www.yestermorrow.org, 888-496-5541).* Offers the three-month natural building intensive in which the garden folly was built, as well as two- to fourteen-day workshops focused on building with straw bale and cob, the use of natural plasters and finishes, timberframe construction, and the installation of green roofs.

COB COTTAGE COMPANY, COQUILLE, OR. *(www.cobcottage.com, 541-396-1825).* Provides workshops in building with cob and rocket stove design and construction, as well as two- to six-month apprenticeship programs.

SOLAR ENERGY INTERNATIONAL, CARBONDALE, CO. *(www.solarenergy.org, 970-963-8866).* Has two- to five-day courses and workshops in building with straw bales, the use of natural plasters, and the integration of renewable energy systems.

Following excavation below frostline, a rubble trench foundation system was laid providing drainage below grade. Atop the rubble, the foundation rises above grade with a stemwall of large flat stones quarried from the immediate site and mortared with a cement-lime mixture. The stem wall needed to be wide enough to comfortably house the 18-inch thick strawbale walls to come above.

Smaller stones were fished from the river. The builders relied as much as possible on materials found locally in nature (stone, earth, clay, timber, straw) and minimized the use of manufactured or processed materials, thus avoiding the use of the chemicals and energy that would otherwise have been outputted.

Following excavation and the laying of a stone foundation, quarried from the immediate site, smaller stones were fished from the river across the road and used to construct its entryway threshold.

(above) Stones fished from a nearby river make for a beautiful transition from outdoors to indoors. (right) Built almost entirely of natural and local materials, the Garden Folly is a testament to low-impact, sustainable building techniques.

Both square rule and scribe timberframing methods create a solid structure that is also a design statement.

▶ RAISING THE FRAME AND WALLS

The frame of the structure was erected next. It is a timberframe, or post and beam, design relying on a hybrid of locally milled square timbers and unmilled round timbers assembled using square rule and scribe methodologies. The joints were cut by hand with saws, chisels, and mortisers, and then raised and joined together with pegs. Not one nail or screw was utilized.

For the walls, or infill between the posts, the students used a variety of techniques and materials, including stacked strawbales, which provide dynamic insulation value; cob, which is a mixture of clay, water, and sand mixed together and fashioned into bricks; and wattle and daub, an ancient technique in which tree branches are woven together into a lattice and covered with a sticky mixture of clay, sand, and chopped straw.

Window and door openings were framed with scrap lumber, and the windows and doors are recycled, sourced at a local materials reuse center. Some wine bottles were inserted in the walls as an artistic element.

To keep water from infiltrating and causing the wall materials to deteriorate, numerous coats of natural plasters and washes were applied to both the interior and exterior. Locally sourced clay- and lime-based plasters were mixed on-site and applied by hand and trowel.

Wine bottles "windows" accent the naturally-sculpted walls.

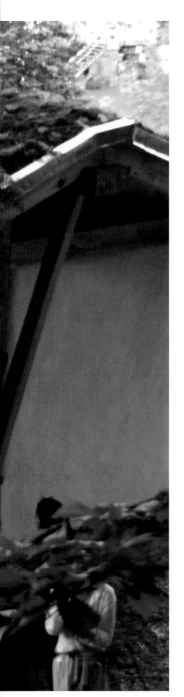

▶ INSTALLING A GREEN ROOF

The folly was capped by a green, or living, roof. Also a traditional building methodology (think Scandinavian sod roofs), green roofs are making a comeback for several reasons: the soil and plants on green roofs act as insulators, they reduce stormwater run-off by catching and holding a large percentage of the rain, they filter pollutants and carbon dioxide out of the air, they reduce temperatures, and they replace lost vegetation and wildlife habitat taken up by the building's footprint.

They can also extend the lifespan of the roof.

Since water is retained for periods of time in the soil, green roofs require an impermeable layer of waterproof material beneath them to keep that moisture from soaking down into the structure beneath. In the case of this folly, the materials used for this membrane were not of natural origin. Additionally, the roof was sheathed with plywood, as its structural strength was needed to support the heavy weight of the growing medium.

▶ THE FINISHING TOUCHES

Lastly, the interior was outfitted with an earthen floor and a cob sitting bench housing the heating flue of a rocket stove. An earthen floor is not the dusty dirt floor you'd imagine. It is actually a combination of dirt, clay and chopped straw, along with a stabilizer such as starch paste or casein. It is compacted and then sealed with linseed or hemp oil. The result can be quite attractive, and the cost minimal.

The rocket stove is the heating source for the structure. Its design provides complete wood combustion and efficient use of the heat that combustion produces. The thermal mass

of the cob bench acts as a long-term radiator, holding and slowly disseminating the warmth for hours at a time.

This structure is more than a showplace of natural building technologies. It has the potential to function year-round as an office, art or writing studio, or guest house, or to serve virtually any other use. And though the techniques used in its construction are not necessarily in the common, contemporary building vernacular, with a little bit of training, they are readily accessible to those who seek to acquire them.

Glossary

AWNING: A type of window that is hinged along the upper edge of the sash and opens out.

BAND (OR RIM) JOIST: A framing member positioned horizontally and on edge on the mudsill around the perimeter of a structure, and supporting the subfloor.

BEARING WALL: A wall that supports joists and other framing above, transferring weight to the foundation below. All exterior walls are bearing, as are some interior walls.

BIRD'S MOUTH: A triangular notch cut into the underside of a rafter so it will sit comfortably on the top plate.

BOARD AND BATTEN: Wood siding wide and narrow boards, with narrower boards sitting atop wider boards to cover the joints between.

BUTT JOINT: Where two square-edged pieces of wood meet.

CASEMENT: A window hinged along a vertical edge that pivots in or out.

CASING: Trim applied around a door or window.

CROSS CUT: A cut running perpendicular to the direction of the wood grain.

CROWN: The higher or bowed edge of a framing member.

DECKING: The material that forms a base for flooring or roofing material.

DOUBLE-HUNG: A window with two sashes, one above the other, where one sash slides behind the other.

EAVE: The horizontal edge of a roof, usually overhanging the wall.

ELEVATION: A two-dimensional rendering of a wall surface, to scale.

FACE-NAILING: Driving a nail through a wood material at right angles to the surface.

FLOOR PLAN: A scaled drawing of a structure's layout looking directly from above.

FLUSH: Perfectly even.

GABLE: The triangular end of a roof.

GAMBREL: A roof comprising four planes and two pitches: the upper two planes at a shallow pitch, the lower two planes at a steep pitch.

HEADER: A piece of framing above a door or window opening in a wall that transfers weight down and around the opening.

JAMB: A board that forms the top or side of a door or window frame.

JOIST: A framing member placed horizontally and on edge, as with a floor or ceiling joist.

KERF: A narrow notch cut partway through a board.

LEVEL: Exactly horizontal.

MITER: An angled cut that is less or more than 90°.

ON CENTER: The distance from the center of a framing member to the center of the next framing member. Usually abbreviated as "o.c."

PLATE: A horizontal framing member lying flat that forms the top or bottom of a wall frame unit.

PLUMB: Exactly vertical.

PRESSURE TREATED (PT): Wood injected with a preservative via intense pressure.

PROUD: Protrude above or beyond; stick out slightly.

RAFTER: An angled framing member that forms part of the sloping sides of a roof.

RAKE: The angled edge of a roof.

RIDGEBOARD: The crest of the roof to which the tops of the rafters are fastened.

RIP CUT: A cut parallel to the direction of the wood grain.

RISE: The vertical distance covered by anything that slopes, including a stairway or a roof.

ROUGH OPENING: An opening in the framing to allow for window or door installation.

RUN: The horizontal distance covered by anything that slopes, including a stairway or a roof.

SASH: The part of a window holding the glass.

SHAKE: A wooden shingle produced by splitting cedar along the grain.

SHEATHING: The exterior skin of a structure under the siding.

SHIPLAP: An edge where each board is milled with an L-shape on the opposite face so it fits into the adjacent board.

SIDING: Any material used as the outer skin of a structure.

SILL: A framing member laying flat and supporting the band joist.

SLIDER: A window with two or more sashes placed horizontally, which is opened by one sash sliding behind another.

SQUARE: A 90° angle at the point where two pieces of lumber meet.

STRINGER: A diagonal piece of lumber supporting a stairway.

STUD: A vertical framing member.

TOENAILING: Driving a nail at an angle.

TONGUE-AND-GROOVE: A milling of boards so that one edge forms a tongue and the other edge is grooved, with the tongue of one board meant to fit snugly into the groove of the adjacent board.

TRUSS: A triangular structural design most often used in roofs to span long distances.

Index

Index

Index

Photo Credits

Burcu Avsar: 174

Neal Barrett: 54 (bottom), 85 (middle), 86 (left), 140 (bottom right), 151

Courtesy of Better Barns, LLC: 27, 32, 51, 71, 98-99 (all photos), 103, 118-119 (all photos), 134, 140 (top)

Bruce Bradford: 143 (bottom)

Brian Berman: 141

Michael Cogliantry: 12, 130, 147, 161

Alessandro Contadini/iStockphoto: 33 (top right)

Kobby Dagan/iStockphoto: 9

Richard deBrasky: 55

Michelle Dulieu/iStockphoto: 110

Dan Eckstein: 43, 82 (right), 102, 105, 176-180 (all photos)

Dustin Feider O2 Treehouse.com: 175

Sharon Foelz/iStockphoto: 132 (right)

Bobbi Gathings/iStockphoto: 21

Randy Gerweck: 140 (bottom left)

Robert Green: 16

Geoffrey Gross: 25, 33 (top left), 54 (top), 81 (both photos), 85 (bottom), 88, 133, 143 (top), 144, 165

Jayme Halbritter/Getty Images: 101

Merle Henkenius: 34-39 (all photos), 54 (two middle photos), 62, 64, 69 (bottom), 80, 82 (bottom left), 85 (top), 106-107 (all photos), 132 (left top and bottom), 136, 157

iStockphoto: 22, 28-29, 41, 44-45, 46-47, 72, 129, 131, 139, 148-149

Tore Johannesen/iStockphoto: 67 (top)

Donald Johansson/iStockphoto: 76-77

Hakan Karlsson/iStockphoto: 126

Russell Kaye: 4

Daniel Kourey/iStockphoto: 90